W9-BKO-529

Edward Payson Roe

Twayne's United States Authors Series

David J. Nordloh, Editor

Indiana University, Bloomington

TUSAS 480

EDWARD PAYSON ROE
(1837–1888)

Edward Payson Roe

By Glenn O. Carey

Eastern Kentucky University

Twayne Publishers • *Boston*

Edward Payson Roe

Glenn O. Carey

Book Production by Elizabeth Todesco
Book Design by Barbara Anderson

Printed on permanent/durable acid-free
paper and bound in the United States of
America.

Library of Congress Cataloging in Publication Data

Carey, Glenn O.
    Edward Payson Roe.

    (Twayne's United States authors series; TUSAS 480)
    Bibliography: p. 111
    Includes index.
    1. Roe, Edward Payson, 1838–1888—Criticism and interpretation.
I. Title.   II. Series.
PS2728.C37   1985   813'.4   84-27962
ISBN 0–8057–7421–1

To Earle Labor,
Katherine Babbitt,
Dennis Minor,
Carolyn Britt,
and Margaret Carey

Contents

About the Author

Glenn O. Carey, professor of English at Eastern Kentucky University, is a graduate of Pennsylvania State University (B.A., M.A.) and the University of Illinois at Urbana-Champaign (Ph.D.).

He has been awarded two Senior Fulbright Lectureships, one, 1965–1966, in American literature at the University of Jordan in Amman; the other, 1976–1977, in American Studies and American literature at the University of Tehran, Iran. In December 1965 he was Visiting Fulbright Lecturer in American literature in Nicosia, Cyprus. He has been an American literature lecturer for the United States Information Agency: during 1965–1966, in Jordan, in Ramallah, Amman, Jerusalem; during 1976–1977, in Iran, in Isfahan, Shiraz, Tehran, Ahwaz; and for the month of April 1977 in India speaking on Faulkner, Whitman, Twain, and Hemingway at the American Studies Research Centre and the India Institute for Advanced Studies, as well as at universities in New Delhi and Hyderabad.

He has edited two books—*Quest for Meaning–Modern Short Stories* (1975) and *Faulkner–the Unappeased Imagination* (1980)—and written thirty articles and three hundred and fifty book reviews, published in journals that include the *Saturday Review, Library Journal, American Quarterly, Military Review, CEA Critic, Arizona Quarterly, Studies in Short Fiction,* and *Journal of English and Germanic Philology.* In 1949–1950 he was an assistant editor of *Accent,* the literary magazine; and from 1968–1973 he presented a weekly Kentucky educational radio program, "Books and Authors, Today and Yesterday."

He served in the United States Army in World War II (1942–1946) and the Korean War (1951–1953), mainly in field artillery. He is a graduate of the Army Command and General Staff College and retired from military service as a lieutenant colonel.

Since 1974 he has been a member of the National American Studies Faculty and since 1975 an elected member of the National Book Critics Circle. In 1974–1975 he was the national president of the College English Association and in 1984 received the National CEA Distinguished Service Award.

Preface

In 1896 Fred Lewis Pattee wrote, "If he is most successful in literature who is most widely popular, and who exerts the most far-reaching influence, then E. P. Roe must be counted among the most successful of American novelists." Pattee, who is often called the first professor of *American* literature in the United States, then added, "Howells and James [and Twain] . . . appeal to the literary connoisseur, to the educated and the cultured; Roe is the novelist of the great middle class which constitutes the reading majority. His novels are singularly fitted to appeal to the class for which they were written." Pattee concluded that Roe's novels cannot be overlooked by the American literary critic and historian, for they must be "counted among the most successful creations of American literature."[1]

From 1871 to at least 1915, and even into the early 1920s, the novels of Edward Payson Roe were the publishing phenomenon of his time. It has been over one hundred years since Roe wrote his first novel, and the fact that an extensive study of this preacher/novelist and his books has not been made until now is a serious failure of American literary scholarship.

In this study I consider all the writings of E. P. Roe, some intensively and extensively, others only in summary or highlight. To assist those who have not read Roe's novels and those who would also have difficulty in obtaining them, I have included plot summaries and character discussions that may seem excessive, perhaps repetitious. But the advantage of having a thorough, almost definitive consideration of Roe in one book will be extremely valuable for research, as well as for the resurrection of his writings and their examination by contemporary scholars.

I believe this thorough method has especially been put to appropriate use in discussing and evaluating the Civil War chronicles of Roe, who was a chaplain in the cavalry during most of this national conflict. Roe's descriptions of battle scenes and his understanding of the inner feelings of soldiers are outstanding. Because his columns in the New York *Evangelist,* where these battlefield reports were originally published, are difficult to obtain, I have included a fairly large number of extracts from these writings in order that readers may have a representative sampling for convenient use. Attention also has been given to Roe's post-Civil War lectures, which he undertook to raise money to build a new church for his parishioners in Highland Falls, New York.

While writing this study of America's "native author," as Matthew Arnold satirically labeled Roe, I have learned to respect and admire Roe the man and to evaluate objectively Roe the author. Within both his life and his writings Roe was a person who followed basic concepts—goodness, kindness, love of mankind—guided by practical and flexible Christian teachings which were not denominational.

Roe personified the best hopes of all men, it seemed, to all who met him. In 1888 Nathaniel Hawthorne's son Julian, in a eulogy of Roe, wrote, "He was so good a man that no one can take his place with those who knew him. It is the simple truth that he cared for his friends more than for himself: that his greatest happiness was to see others happy: that he would have more rejoiced in the literary fame of one of his friends than in any such fame of his own winning," for "he was at once manly and childlike: manly in honor, truth and tenderness; childlike in the simplicity that suspects no guile and practises none."[2]

What Julian Hawthorne wrote about his friend when Roe unexpectedly died in July 1888, was echoed by many people who wrote to publications throughout the United States. Edward Roberts commented, "Mr. Roe was loved there [in Cornwall-on-the Hudson, where Roe lived a large portion of his life] because he deserved to be. It may not be generally known that all profits from his earlier novels and writings were given to the payment of debts contracted by another. And yet such is the fact. Mr. Roe was not a rich man, though he might have been." Before Roe became a famous and successful author whose name caused phenomenal sales, as Frank Luther Mott in *Golden Multitudes* has verified, he endorsed the investments of his brother. "While yet unknown to fame[,]" Roberts continued, "his endorsement of certain notes threw him into bankruptcy. Soon after, his reputation was made; but every dollar earned was given to creditors who legally could not have collected a cent. The money was given cheerfully; and it amounted to a large sum. . . ."[3]

In the 1870s, 1880s, and 1890s Roe's books were being printed in editions of twenty, thirty, one hundred thousand— and selling rapidly and steadily not only upon original publication but ten to thirty years later. This amazing accomplishment— mainly, it appears, as the result of the best advertising of all, word-of-mouth recommendations from one reader to another— reached such a zenith in 1888 that Paul R. Cleveland could reliably remark: "Financially he is a giant among lilliputians as to manuscript-making. It sounds incredible, but I am authoritively informed that the royalty from his works for the last fiscal year reached forty thousand dollars. . . ."[4]

These aspects of Roe's life and writings are considered in this study, which I hope will bring about a renewed interest in Roe—the man Matthew Arnold, without realizing it, accurately called America's native author. For, if ever an American author was a people's writer, it certainly was E. P. Roe. The time is long overdue for American literary critics to examine the writings of Edward Payson Roe.

Over twenty years ago I began my interest in E. P. Roe, collecting his novels and other books at country auctions, Salvation Army and Goodwill Industry retail outlets, and rummage sales. It was Professor Earle Labor who suggested this study of Roe, and thanks to his encouragement and urging I wrote to Dr. Sylvia Bowman, then senior editor for Twayne United States Authors Series. Further thanks are due to John LaBine, Alice Phalen, and Emily McKeigue of Twayne Publishers, as well as to Dr. David J. Nordloh, editor of this volume, and Lewis DeSimone, Twayne manuscript editor.

There were also responses to my nationally published inquiries about Roe's life. I received replies from several researchers, including one from Dr. Dennis E. Minor, whose findings on Roe's letters and Civil War dispatches to the New York *Evangelist* he generously shared with me. But an even greater appreciation has to be given to Katherine M. Babbitt of Highland Falls, New York, the town where Roe preached and wrote. She, like Professor Minor, has voluntarily shared her extensive bibliographic and other research. Also among those to whom I am deeply grateful is my former secretary, Carolyn Britt, who has typed the entire manuscript.

My appreciation goes also to Eastern Kentucky University for the university research grant I received during 1979. This timely grant enabled me to use Roe research materials in New York City and Highland Falls, New York. The library staff at Eastern Kentucky University has been particularly helpful. My warm thanks goes to these friends and colleagues there: Librarian Ernest E. Weyhrauch, Dean of Libraries and Learning Resources; Mary John Thurman (now retired), Paul Fritts, George Crabb, Peggy Flaherty, and Rebecca Turner, Reference Librarians; June Martin and Marie Brewer, Circulation Librarians; Genevieve Clay, Mary Anne Dewey, and Ledell Curry, Periodicals Librarians; and Ken Barksdale, Acquisitions Librarian. Paul W. Lambert in the Public Information Division, and Larry D. Moberly, Director of Printing Services, both at Eastern Kentucky University, also assisted me.

At the New York Public Library, Walter Zervas graciously facilitated my research. At the New York Historical Society, James Gregory and Mary Tomasek made my research pleasantly profitable. I also thank Professor Cleanth Brooks for his advice about the poem by Vachel Lindsay, "John L. Sullivan, the Strong Boy of Boston." I thank the Macmillan Company for granting me permission to quote from this poem and I also thank the Bowdoin College Library for permitting me to quote an E. P. Roe letter to Lyman Abbott. My gratitude goes to the Reverend Harry Revel, Richmond, Kentucky, and Ann Egerton, Nashville, Tennessee, for their efforts to locate Roe books for my personal library.

I have also been fortunate to have been aided by living relatives of E. P. Roe, including Mrs. Julie C. Tatham, Dr. Eddison C. Tatham, Mrs. James C. Jacobson, and Professor Campbell Tatham, all of whom were full of encouragement for my Roe enterprise. Their friendly generosity would have pleased E. P. Roe. I thank also Professors Kelly Thurman and Donald R. Swanson who wholeheartedly supported my early Roe research. As usual, my warmest thanks are for Margaret Carey, my wife.

Glenn O. Carey

Eastern Kentucky University

Chronology

1880 *Success with Small Fruits. A Day of Fate.*
1881 *Without a Home.*
1882 *Birthday Mottoes* ("The Roe Birthday Book").
1883 *An Unexpected Result and Other Stories.*
1884 *A Young Girl's Wooing.*
1885 *Nature's Serial Story. An Original Belle. Driven Back to Eden.*
1886 *He Fell in Love with His Wife. The Hornet's Nest.*
1887 *The Earth Trembled.*
1888 *Queen of Spades.* " 'A Native Author Called Roe' " (autobiography). *Found Yet Lost.* Dies from stroke, 11 July, leaving his wife Anna and five children. *"Miss Lou"* (unfinished novel).
1889 *The Home Acre. Taken Alive and Other Stories.*
1892 *A Brave Little Quakeress and Other Stories.*
1894 Roe Park dedicated at Cornwall-on-Hudson, New York.

Chapter One
America's "Native Author"
Time and Reputation

When in 1888 Edward Payson Roe wrote his brief autobiography, " 'A Native Author Called Roe' "—taking his title from a condemnatory essay written by Matthew Arnold—he did not realize that he was also writing his own obituary. Death occurred suddenly and unexpectedly three weeks after Roe had completed his memoir: he suffered a severe heart attack and died within a few hours at his home in Cornwall, upstate New York, while reading to his family from a book by Nathaniel Hawthorne, one of Roe's favorite authors.

In this short autobiography, only eighteen pages, and delayed in the writing because of his inherent modesty until several years after the editors of *Lippincott's Magazine* had requested it, Roe declared his professional and personal principles: "An author should maintain completely and thoroughly his own individuality and take the consequences. He cannot conjure strongly by imitating anyone, or by representing any school or fashion. He must do his work conscientiously, for his readers know by instinct whether or not they are treated seriously and with respect. Above all, he must understand men and women sufficiently to interest them; for all the 'powers that be' cannot compel them to read a book they do not like."[1] Roe understood men and women more than sufficiently to be able to write novels that captured their interest. His readers liked his books so much and bought so many, as sales figures attest, that Roe became one of America's best-selling novelists, the undisputed leader in total book sales from 1872 to 1888, with unusually large sales continuing at least to 1910. As Katherine M. Babbitt has discovered through her extensive bibliographic research, Roe's books went on being read many years after his death; seven editions of his collected works were issued between 1890 and

1912, most of them by subscription.[2] In 1910 George Middleton's dramatization of *Barriers Burned Away* had a successful
opening at the Bijou Opera House in Minneapolis, Minnesota.
In 1925, as Babbitt relates, Grosset and Dunlap published *Barriers Burned Away* and illustrated it with scenes taken from a photoplay based on the novel. Two more reprints of *Barriers Burned
Away* were published in 1970.[3]

When Edward Payson Roe died in 1888 at the age of fifty-
one, he had written many best-selling novels and several well-
received books on home gardening. Throughout his fiction he
had tried consistently to maintain his own individuality and not
imitate any author or represent any school or fashion. Surprisingly, even after his death, his books, including *Barriers Burned
Away,* his first novel, continued to sell in exceptional numbers.
At the same time that Roe was writing and publishing, Lew
Wallace's *Ben Hur* was a popular novel; and even though Mark
Twain, William Dean Howells, and Henry James were also
writing during the last decades of the nineteenth century, their
novels were not selling as Roe's were. Vachel Lindsay in "John
L. Sullivan, the Strong Boy of Boston" (1889) noted Roe's
remarkable popularity as a novelist. The beginning of Lindsay's
poem provides a condensed historical, sociological, and literary
glimpse of the period when Roe wrote:

> When I was nine years old, in 1889,
> I sent my love a lacy Valentine.
> Suffering boys were dressed like Fauntleroys,
> While Judge and Puck in giant humor vied.
> The Gibson Girl came shining like a bride
> To spoil the cult of Tennyson's Elaine.
> Louisa Alcott was my gentle guide. . . .
> Then . . .
> I heard a battle trumpet sound.
> Nigh New Orleans
> Upon an emerald plain
> John L. Sullivan
> The strong boy
> Of Boston
> Fought seventy-five red rounds with Jake Kilrain.
>
> In simple sheltered 1889
> Nick Carter I would piously deride.

Over the Elsie Books I moped and sighed.
St. Nicholas Magazine was all my pride,
While coarser boys in cellar doors would slide.
The grown-ups bought refinement by the pound.
Rogers groups had not been told to hide.
E. P. Roe had just begun to wane.
Howells was rising, surely to attain!
The nation for a jamboree was gowned.—
Her hundredth year of roaring freedom crowned.[4]

From 1872 through 1888 and for at least twenty years after his death Roe received extraordinary approval from the American reading public who bought his books by the millions. Unlike Harold Bell Wright (1872–1944), who was among the first American authors to use a well-organized national advertising campaign to sell novels, Roe usually found first publication for his novels in serial form in a periodical. When the novels were later published as books they sold in what then were unbelievable numbers because, as Frank Luther Mott has written in *Golden Multitudes,* Roe's "name was magic."[5] A conservative estimate of the sales of Roe's books in the United States and only by Dodd & Mead, his original publisher, would be five million copies, a phenomenal figure for the last decade of the nineteenth century. Many of his novels were also published in England, some of them in pirated editions, and the sales there were also unusually high. When Roe died, *Publishers Weekly* in its obituary referred to him as "for the last ten years the most widely-read American author."[6] *Harper's Bazar* also praised Roe: "Another popular benefactor in the way of every-day literature has passed away. 'A native author called Roe' is the way in which he was condescendingly described not long since by Mr. [Matthew] Arnold; but he was dear, and justly dear, to multitudes of sensible persons who had never heard of his critic, and who obtained from their favorite novelist a store of cheer and courage which that critic did not always bestow on the human race."[7]

When Roe wrote his short autobiography for *Lippincott's Magazine* he rebutted the cynical criticism of Matthew Arnold, who wrote that "the Western States are at this moment being nourished and formed, we hear, on novels of a native author called Roe, instead of those by Scott and Dickens."[8] Roe's reply included the salient observation that he was just one author among many whose books were sold in the United States, including those by British authors such as Dickens whose novels were pirated by American publishers because of the total lack of copyright protection. To Roe, "tons of such novels have been sold annually in the West, a thousand to one of the '[native] author called Roe' " (*NA*, 490).

Roe also admonished the United States Congress for not providing a copyright law for both American and foreign authors. (In 1891, three years after Roe's death, the International Copyright Act was passed, protecting rights of foreign authors and publishers.) He also asked why Matthew Arnold, when he was traveling in America, had not taken "a few moments to look into the bookstores of the great cities of the West, in order to have observed for himself how the demand of one of the largest and most intelligent reading publics in the world is supplied." If Arnold had asked, Roe stated, "he would have found that the works of Scott and Dickens were more liberally purchased and generally read than in his own land of 'distinction,' " because "he should have discovered when in this country that American statesmen (?) are so solicitous about the intelligence of their constituents that they give publishers so disposed every opportunity to steal novels describing the nobility and English persons of distinction." Besides excoriatingly condemning the lack of copyright laws for writers in the United States, England, Canada, and elsewhere in the world, as he did throughout his writing career, Roe also spoke about the reasons his novels sold so astonishingly well: "The simple truth in the case is that, in spite of this immense and cheap competition, my novels have made their way and are being read among multitudes of others." Roe left the question of the value of his work to his audience: "No one buys or reads a book under compulsion; and if any one thinks that the poorer the book the better the chance of its being read by the American people, let him try the experiment. When a critic condemns my books, I accept that as his judgment; when another critic and scores of men and women, the peers of the first in cultivation and intelligence, commend the books, I do not charge them with gratuitous lying" (*NA*, 490).

As a modern-day critic examines the publication and sales figures of American novels in the last three decades of the nineteenth century, it soon becomes apparent—and for most American critics surprisingly so—that there is an overdue necessity to analyze and evaluate Roe's novels so that we may understand why his writings had such a vast appeal. It has been over one hundred years since Roe wrote his first novel, and today many aspects of critical taste and judgment have changed. In order to appraise his fiction, two periods of critical evaluation and judgment need to be applied—the late 1800s and the late 1900s.

E. P. Roe was a many-sided individual—an outstanding minister and Civil War chaplain, a superior horticulturist, a self-taught writer, and an unusually good man. Within his memoir can be found his consistent awareness that time alone should eventually provide the definitive assessment of his and any other author's writing: he was more than willing to accept that inexorable judgment. As he wrote in "A Native Author Called Roe," "My one aim has become to do my work conscientiously and leave the final verdict to time and the public. I wish no other estimate than a correct one; and when the public indicate that they have had enough of Roe I shall neither whine nor write." He also wrote that "over twelve years ago, certain oracles, with the voice of fate, predicted my speedy eclipse and disappearance." But he resolutely restated his belief in the final judgment by time: "My active life brought me in close contact with all kinds of people. . . . I at least know the nature that exists in the human breast. It may be inartistic, or my use of it all wrong. That is a question which time will decide, and I shall accept the verdict" (*NA,* 490).

Family and Home

Besides including in " 'A Native Author Called Roe' " a vigorous reply to Matthew Arnold and a denunciation of the United States Congress for not legislating copyright laws, E. P. Roe gave some information about his life as a boy, youth, and man. His younger sister Mary Abigail Roe in 1899 provided more details about her brother's life and writing career in a 157-page biography, *E. P. Roe, Reminiscences of His Life.* As she wrote in her "Introductory Note," "Since the death of Edward Payson Roe, in 1888, there have been inquiries from time to time for some record of his life and work, and it is in response to these repeated requests that this volume is issued."[9] In an unpublished diary Roe's older sister Susan also wrote about the Roe family and her famous brother, Edward.

The Roe family lived in a roomy farm-style home in a rural community in upstate New York. Edward, Mary, and Susan Roe wrote with much love and pleasant memories of their childhood in Moodna (now New Windsor in Orange County), New York, a few miles south of Newburgh and just west of the Hudson River. For Susan, "It was a home of peace and happiness as far as I remember."[10] As nostalgically described by the three of them, life in the Roe family was close to idyllic, with young Edward growing up under the concatenated influences of his mother and father, God and nature. That these were continuing influences on Roe is evident in the obituary E. D. Walker wrote in the September 1888, *Cosmopolitan:* "Mr. Roe's home at Cornwall-on-the-Hudson is a pretty country seat, and was much loved by him. He was essentially a domestic man, preferring the family hearthstone to the honors literary friends were always ready to heap upon him and caring little for fame." Walker continued, comparing Roe to George MacDonald, the Scottish minister/writer: "The warm love of home-life springs forth in all of his stories. Like George Macdonald [*sic*], he believed that 'Homeliness and glory make heaven.' With what affection he held domestic ties one may see clearly in the opening words of 'Nature's Serial Story,' which is more closely autobiographical than his other works. In the delightful old couple there pictured are his own mother and father, and the other members of the group are chiefly composed from his near kindred and friends."[11]

Edward Payson Roe was born on 7 March 1837, the seventh child of Peter and Susan Roe. Susan Roe, née Williams, was the daughter of Jonas Williams of Cornwall, who had moved there from Long Island during the American Revolution. Peter and Susan Roe had eight children: Oswald W. (who died when still a young child), Alfred C., James G., Susan E., William W., Peter, Edward P., and Mary A. His father was forty-nine when Edward was born, for he had lived in New York City for many years before settling in Moodna and marrying. In the city he had worked with his uncle, William Roe, who had been employed by John Jacob Astor and later had become a highly successful wholesale grocer and importer. In 1826 he moved to Newburgh with what the history of Newburg calls an ample fortune. There he eventually became president of the Newburgh Whaling Company.

Although Peter Roe was apparently not so successful in business as his Uncle William, when he settled in Moodna he had a comfortable income. Both William and Peter Roe had been born in Kingston, New York, and the north country of New York state had much appeal for them, just as it later had for Edward Payson, Peter's son. Edward, the man, remembered his father as a "sturdy man of action" whose love for the country was so strong that he retired from business as soon as he had a "modest competence." Peter Roe left many lasting impressions on his son, Edward, including a love of nature and the land, instilling in his boy positive habits of thinking fortified by staunchness of purpose. The father was "simple and positive in his beliefs, always openly foremost in the reform movements of his day and in his neighborhood" (*NA,* 480). The history of Newburgh reports that Peter Roe had garnered a reputation as the first abolitionist of Orange County and that before the Civil War he had used his home as a station of the Underground Railroad. Edward vividly remembered a dangerous incident when his father helped a slave to escape to Canada: "One night in the depth of winter he took a hotly-pursued fugitive in his sleigh and drove him five miles on the ice, diagonally across the Hudson, to Fishkill, thence putting the brave aspirant for freedom on the way to other friends. He incurred several risks in this act. It is rarely safe to drive on the river off the beaten tracks at night, for there are usually air-holes, and the strong tides are continually making changes in the ice. When told that he might be sent to jail for his defiance of the Fugitive Slave Law, he quietly answered, 'I can go to jail.' The thing he could not do was to deny the man's appeal to him for help" (*NA,* 481).

The mature Edward frequently described his father as a man consistently simple, direct, and honorable in his beliefs and actions; and these standards of integrity were inculcated in the young boy, particularly when he saw his father's steadfast position on matters of principle. Susan Roe also wrote that their father was no coward. In her diary she praised him for his intelligence, his use of excellent English (despite having a somewhat limited education), and his library, which was particularly stocked with books of poetry and history. Even when a young child, Susan was impressed by her father's demeanor and appearance, personal characteristics that observers also noted in his son Edward.

From his mother too Roe received an abundance of love and guidance; like her husband, she gave her son lifelong interests. Edward, Mary, and Susan all remember their mother as an unusually capable woman, even though all during their lives she was an invalid. As Edward wrote, "My mother died some years before I attained my majority, and I cannot remember when she was not an invalid" (*NA*, 480). Susan explained, "She was an invalid most of her married life mostly due to wrong medical treatment." Like Peter Roe, his wife made extra efforts with her clothes and appearance, as their daughter Susan noted: "Although Mother was an invalid and had to lie on the bed or sofa most of her time, she was always neatly and prettily dressed, wearing soft thread lace caps. She liked embroidery on her underclothes, wore slippers and pretty open-worked stockings."[12]

To assist Mrs. Roe with her household and familial duties, Mr. Roe hired an old black cook, a wet nurse named Mam Bond, and a housekeeper named Betsey Williams. "Betsey was never a servant, but a valued friend," Susan Roe wrote.[13] The cook's husband was the gardener. Earlier there had been a governess: Miss Woodham, an English lady, was with the Roe family several years. From her the Roe children received their earliest education. Susan wrote that Edward "was full of mischief when very little and tried Betsey's patience. When it gave out, she picked him up and carried him to Mother's room and sat him down beside the bed, and laid a little whip on it. Mother was too weak to use the whip but it represented authority. He would puff and blow till he quieted down, then Mother told him stories."[14] Mary Roe observed that the Roe home was always full of "generous hospitality"[15] and that there were frequent guests and visitors, for Mrs. Roe was a superior conversationalist. Lawyers and clergymen who were her friends often came to discuss religion, books, politics, and current events.

Edward Roe, when he was fifty years old and writing his brief autobiography, easily remembered his mother's sharp mind and wide reading interests: "Such literary tendencies as I have are derived from her, but I do not possess a tithe of her intellectual power. Her story-books in her youth were the classics; and when she was but twelve years of age she knew 'Paradise Lost' by heart. In my recollections of her the Bible and all works tending to elucidate its prophecies were her favorite themes of study. The retentiveness of her memory was very remarkable." Mrs. Roe also enjoyed travel and history. "Confined usually to her room, she took unfailing delight in wandering about the world with the great travellers of that day, her strong fancy reproducing the scenes they described" (*NA,* 480). As a boy, Edward saw his mother's excitement from what she was reading, noting her "flushed cheeks and sparkling black eyes" in spite of her frail health. "The [travel] works of Hugh Miller [1802–1856] and the Arctic Explorations of Dr. [Elisha Kent] Kane [1820–1857] afforded her much pleasure," and "a stirring bit of history moved her deeply." Young Edward was indelibly marked by her capacity to explicate, for "she had the unusual gift of relating in an easy, simple way what she read, and many a book far too abstruse and dull for my boyish taste became an absorbing story from her lips" (*NA,* 480).

Through his family came Roe's appreciation of his colonial heritage and especially the ancestors who were involved in the making of American independence. Near the old house where Mrs. Roe had been born, as Mary relates, "was a mound of cinders marking the spot where once stood the forge upon which our grandfather wrought the great iron chain which was stretched across the Hudson for the purpose of keeping British ships from sailing beyond it. Some links of this chain are now kept as relics in the Washington 'Headquarters' at Newburgh [New York]."[16] Edward too wrote about his American ancestors: "My forefathers (not 'rude' to my knowledge) were among the first settlers on the Atlantic seaboard. My paternal and maternal grandfathers were staunch Whigs during the Revolution, and had the courage of their convictions. My grandmother escaped with her children from the village of Kingston almost as the British entered it and her home was soon in ashes" (*NA,* 479). In his novels Roe frequently included humorous events, comical characters who often spoke a dialect, and numerous puns, repartee of young men and women—much of this factual material taken from his mother's stories of her family in the colonial period.

The most inclusive summary of the important influence parents and home had on the Roe children can be seen in the concluding paragraph of Susan's diary: "I hardly know if I have felt more pain or pleasure in recalling the old Valley Home, and its inmates. My father and mother were not common people. I do not mean with regard to what most people value, money and such things. They had a higher standard. Father was practical and yet had a great deal of sentiment, like not cutting down the locusts." Mr. Roe had been offered what was then a high price, fifty dollars, for each of the twenty-five tall, straight locust trees around the house (the trees to be used in shipbuilding), but he refused the offer because the trees gave so much beauty to the homestead. "Beauty was more than money. With Father, if anything was right that was enough. There was no temporizing with evil. Dear little Mother was spotless as an angel, but she was always afraid she might come short of the Pearly Gates."[17]

Near the end of her diary Susan wished that their family life could be lived once more—"to live one of those days over and to see old Father come up from the garden with his hoe on his shoulder." For Susan, Mary, and Edward Roe, the influences of their home and parents lasted all their lives, and what Susan wrote was said directly or implied by all three of them, "Those . . . days—it often seems to me Heaven cannot be sweeter."[18]

Boy and Young Man

Susan Roe in her diary makes an early observation about her brother Edward and his first response to religious teaching: "He did not love to go to church and always had a stomachache, which disappeared when the carriage was out of sight."[19] Looking backward in 1888, Edward Payson Roe wrote that he would always remember the religious influence of his mother and, because of her, his first acquaintance with the Bible (NA, 480). As has been mentioned, clergymen often came to discuss with Mrs. Roe the latest developments in current events, politics, and religion. Both Mr. and Mrs. Roe encouraged their children to talk about ideas and things, not people. During visits to Moodna, for example, Dr. Samuel Cox sometimes gave public lectures and sermons in the region. In one of his talks he presented a radical conjecture, which, besides indicating his progressive views about religion, also illustrates Peter Roe's religious toleration and rational perspective on unusual religious interpretations. Susan Roe wrote: "Dr. Cox in lecturing said Christ was dark, a colored man. It was taken up by all the papers and a great row made. (Likely now it is forgotten as if never said.) Dr. Cox was staying at our house and was to lecture at the Dutch Reformed Church in Newburgh. I do not remember his subject, but this saying of his was bruited about by the 'baser sort' and a crowd of them mobbed the church. Father took the doctor out by a side door, [and they] went through my Uncle William Roe's grounds down bystreets to the ferry to Fishkill. I think from there he went to New York. There were always the 'baser sort' in Newburgh; during the Civil War, time of the riots, they caught a man and hung him on Grand Street because he had a black skin."[20]

Just as with religion, both the Roe parents gave their children a love of nature and to Edward the added pleasure of becoming an accomplished amateur horticulturist. In many ways what Ralph Waldo Emerson said in "Nature," that "nature never became a toy to a wise spirit," is true about Edward Payson Roe. Mary believed that "Edward's love of nature was inherited from both Father and Mother. Often, on lovely June days, he would draw Mother's wheeled chair through the broad walks of our large square garden, where the borders on either side were gorgeous with flowers, while I gathered and piled the fragrant blossoms on her lap until she was fairly embowered. Yet one scarcely missed those that were plucked."[21] Like his son Edward, Peter Roe loved nature and her wonders, as Edward frequently remembered: "I observed that my father's interest in his garden and farm never flagged, thus proving that in them is to be found a pleasure that does not pall with age. During the last summer of his life, when in his eighty-seventh year, he had the delight of a child in driving over to my home in the early morning, long before I was up, and in leaving a basket of sweet corn or some other vegetable which he knew would prove his garden to be ahead of mine" (*NA*, 480).

Mrs. Roe too loved growing plants, with roses her favorite.

In " 'A Native Author Called Roe,' " her son wrote, "I can scarcely recall her when a flower of some kind, usually a rose, was not within her reach; and only periods of great feebleness kept her from their daily care, winter and summer" (*NA,* 480). The lasting results of nature on the boy can be seen in the adult, not only in his interest in nature but also in his garden, where he made frequent experiments in horticulture, especially with strawberries. He also wrote several books on horticulture, expertly done and professionally acclaimed, and in his fiction are bountiful examples of comparisons, contrasts, similes, and metaphors—all drawn from nature.

E. D. Walker, in one of the obituaries written on Roe's death, extolled his generosity to his guests and his never-ceasing love of nature: "Mr. Roe was personally one of the most charming of men. His amiable disposition and courteous manner endeared him to all who were so fortunate as to enter the wide circle of his friendship. With his wife and five children he dispensed a charming and bounteous hospitality at his Cornwall home. Among his latest guests were his fellow-members of the Authors' Club, of New York, who were a few weeks ago invited to spend a day at his place. There they found a tall, handsome gentleman, his face beaming with benevolence, though somewhat pale, with long full beard and dark eyes. With open-hearted cordiality he introduced them to his fruits and flowers. Specially beautiful were his favorite roses, to which he devoted much care. The day he selected was in the height of the strawberry season, and the thirty sedate authors of the metropolis reveled among the luscious and gigantic berries, like boys in a melon patch."[22] Just as his parents had done when he was a boy, Edward their son shared the harvest of his garden and unstintingly shared his home, for guests were always welcome.

As can be seen, Edward Payson Roe was influenced by his mother and father in significant ways—through character traits that demonstrated kindness and generosity, through the love of nature and the rewarding pleasures of encouraging the land to bear harvests, and the acceptance of the guiding hand of God. Although there were many laudatory expressions of sympathetic friendship in the obituaries about Roe, the one in *Lippincott's Monthly* by William S. Walsh (who had asked Roe to write his autobiography), sums up the endearing and sincere expressions about the kind of man that the boy had become, who, by combining his love for nature, man, and God, exhibited his goodness of heart and strength of character in his everyday life as well as his endeavors as minister and writer. "Few men, indeed, could meet Mr. Roe without yielding him the tribute of their affection. Fewer still could see him in his own home, moving among his relations, his neighbors, and his friends, could note his unfailing kindliness and sweetness of disposition at the very moment when pain and disease perhaps had claimed him for their own, without rejoicing in the prosperity that crowned his latter years. The money he made from his books he spent with princely generosity."[23] Walsh remarked—as did others—that there was not another author in America who had been so financially successful as Roe. But he noted that Roe's "purse was ever at the command of the poor and the afflicted, his hospitable doors were open to the world. One day a meeting of fellow-authors crowded his house, the next a party of divinity students or of hard-worked preachers found there needed rest and recuperation. His favorite strawberry-beds were the temporary property of his visitors, his horses and carriages were at all hours of the day ready to convey them through his grounds or over the neighboring roads that commanded the most exquisite views."[24]

If ever any boy grew up to be a Christlike man, Edward Roe could have been he, for Roe's entire life from boyhood to manhood is the personification of love for one's fellowman guided by practical Christian teachings. It becomes clearly apparent that he made every effort to include these qualities of character in the themes of his novels.

Call to the Ministry—and Writing

Roe received a great deal of his education at home from his mother and father, as well as from the relatives and other visitors who came to the Roe home. Besides this knowledge about literature, nature, and religion, he received an excellent formal education, although shortened because of ill health.

From his mother, young Edward learned history and the classics of literature, such as *Paradise Lost.* From his mother too came an amazingly thorough knowledge of the Bible. From

Dr. Samuel Cox and other guests at the Roe home, Edward learned about the *Iliad,* the military exploits of Hannibal, and Roman history.

The Roe children at first had a governess who taught them at home, but Edward does not mention these at-home lessons. Susan remembered them vividly, and sometimes with much pain. "I wept over my sewing and lessons. Learning was not made pleasant in those days. My inclinations were to play."[25] Mary wrote about the children's earliest formal schooling, though it was still, in a sense, within the family. "The first school Edward and I attended was a private one for boys and girls kept by our eldest brother, Alfred, in the village of Canterbury, two miles distant from our home."[26] During these days at Alfred Roe's school, Edward Payson Roe and A. Moss Merwin became good friends, and their friendship lasted a lifetime. During this period Roe decided to become a minister. The earliest recollection of this choice of career comes from the adult Merwin, who, when he wrote about his memories of Roe, was a minister in Pasadena, California: "In the little Presbyterian Church near the school, planted mainly through the exertions of his father and elder brothers, there came a time of special religious interest when Edward was deeply impressed. With loving purpose he sought out two of his most intimate companions, and through his instrumentality they then began the Christian life.[27]

Roe was later sent to boarding school to prepare for college, and then enrolled at Williams College in Williamstown, Massachusetts, where his friend Merwin saw Edward as a "fair scholar" who was "more intent at getting at the meaning of the text, and its mythological and historical relations, than in making what is called a fair recitation."[28] While at Williams College, Roe's abilities as a beginning writer and speaker no doubt impressed his classmates; they elected him speaker for the class at a Washington's birthday banquet.

Near the end of his first year at Williams College, Roe had serious problems with his eyesight: "Studying by defective light injured my eyes. They quickly became so sensitive that I could scarcely endure lamplight, or the heat of a stove, only the cold out-door air relieving the pain" (*NA,* 481). As a result he frequently took long walks in the "boisterous [spring] weather" of Williamstown. Finally the troubled young man, exceptionally conscientious (as he was all his life), at the end of his freshman year decided to ask the college's president for advice. The president of Williams College then was Mark Hopkins (1802–1887), the well-known American educator, who made an unusual decision. The mature Roe fondly remembered their interview: "At last I became so discouraged that I went to President Hopkins and told him I feared I must give up the purpose of acquiring an education. Never can I forget how that grand old man met the disheartened boy. Speaking in the wise, friendly way which subdued the heart and strengthened the will, he made the half-hour spent with him the turning-point of my life. . . . He advised me to enter the Senior class the following fall, thus taking a partial course of study. How many men are living to-day who owe much of the best in their lives to that divinely-inspired guide and teacher of youth!" (*NA,* 481–82).

The troubled Roe then consulted with an oculist, who informed him that rest and outdoor living would restore his sight. The diagnosis and treatment were correct, as Roe has written, and the following autumn he entered Williams College again, this time in the class of 1861, spending a happy year there: "Some of my class-mates were very kind in reading aloud to me, and Dr. Hopkins's instruction was invaluable" (*NA,* 482). Although Roe completed only two years at Williams, "the authorities," Merwin has chronicled, "in view of his subsequent success as a writer, gave him his diploma."[29]

After leaving Williams College, Roe entered Auburn Theological Seminary, being able to complete the first year of classes there without further eye problems. In the summer of 1862 he was ordained at Somers, New York, in the North River Presbytery. During Roe's year at Auburn Theological Seminary the Civil War had begun on 12 April 1861. By the summer of 1862, as Roe recollected, "I could no longer resist the call for men in the army" (*NA,* 482).

Chaplain for the Troops

Roe believed it was his duty to enlist as a chaplain in the Northern army. It was a time of heartfelt emotions for him, and the intensity of his thinking about the war and his responsibility to get into uniform have been well recorded by his sister

Mary. His decision to enter the war as a chaplain reached a
climax when he and another man and their two young ladies
were rowing on the Hudson River. (Anna Sands, whom Roe
was escorting that night, became his wife in November 1863.)
When the couples returned to the dock they immediately read
the latest reports about the war in the evening newspapers.
The lead story was about the battle of Bull Run, fought the
previous day. Mary Roe wrote: "I remember Edward's intense
excitement on his return home that night, and his remark that
if he were only through his seminary course he would join
the army as chaplain. From that time I believe the purpose
was constantly in his mind; and the next year, 1862, although
his studies were not then completed, he became chaplain of
the famous Harris Light Cavalry, under the command of the
gallant Kilpatrick, later Brigadier and Major-General, who was
always my brother's firm friend."[30]

Roe felt he could no longer deny his desire to do his duty.
After he learned that the regiment under Lieutenant Colonel
Kilpatrick was without a chaplain, he obtained the appointment
to that position. During his time in service Chaplain Roe, as
he did throughout all his life, devoted himself selflessly to the
welfare of others, profoundly moved by the tragedies caused
by armed conflict, yet becoming actively involved in the most
dangerous battles and campaign maneuvers. During these war
years, when free time was at a minimum, and Roe the chaplain
was giving so much of himself in offering solace and guidance
to the troops, Roe the writer began to emerge: he became a
field correspondent for the New York *Evangelist.*

Not only did Roe write many weekly battlefield reports for
the *Evangelist,* but his outstanding actions as chaplain as well
as his bravery in battle were commended. The New York *Tribune* wrote: "Chaplain Roe, of the Second New York (Harris
Light) Cavalry, is a man whose praises are in the mouth of
every one for his kindly and efficient services. He is always
with the regiment, and his whole time is devoted to the temporal
and spiritual welfare of the men. He is their friend, advisor,
and counsellor, and commands the respect of all who know
him—something that cannot be said of every chaplain in the
army."[31] The *Observer* published a letter about Chaplain Roe
from a Private "S" of the Harris Light Cavalry Regiment to
his parents:

To-day is Sunday, and, as a great exception, it has appeared like Sunday. This morning we had service at headquarters, the chaplain of our regiment officiating, and I think I can safely call him a pious army chaplain, which I cannot say of any others that *I* ever knew; and notwithstanding the little respect most chaplains have shown to them, and still less encouragement, this one, by his mild, gentle, manly, humble, and Christian-like demeanor, has won the respect of all with whom he has had intercourse, from the most profane and vulgar to the most gentlemanly, which few chaplains have been able to do. In a fight he is seen encouraging the men; in the hospital administering to the soldier's wants, both spiritually and bodily. Last winter, during the worst days of a Virginia winter, I have seen him going from camp to camp, distributing his books and papers; and with his own earnings he would buy delicacies that a poor sick soldier would otherwise in vain long for. These and other innumerable like acts have gradually caused every one to at least respect him, and some to love him. His name is Rev. E. P. Roe, Chaplain Harris Light Cavalry . . . If you had any idea what a chaplain had to contend with, in order to lead a consistent life, you might then understand why I speak so of him."[32]

Battle Pieces

Just as Roe's character matured during his chaplaincy, his combat writings provided him with the apprenticeship he needed to write his many popular and successful novels. Roe's Civil War chronicles, which are now difficult to obtain, are worth close attention. They show acute powers of observation and an artistic concern for realistic and accurate details and background information. They also reflect Roe's capacity as a writer to give style and pace to his narratives, whether he is describing a muddy, peaceful campsite or the chaotic conflict of battle. These excellently written battlefield pieces are a highly significant portion of Roe's professional writing career. In some ways, they are as important as his famous novels, presaging certain characteristics—particularly the effective use of description—of his later fiction.

One of his early reports to the *Evangelist* describes a prayer meeting. Because the weather was warm and pleasant with the nights moonlit, he had been holding such meetings every night: "As usual, a large fire was kindled in front of the chaplain's tent, and the men, having disposed of their suppers, were beginning to assemble. Soon the musical 'church-call' sounded to hasten the lagging ones, and by the time our exercises commenced about two hundred were present. Our meetings are of a free and general character, open to all who are willing to take part in them." In describing that night, Roe unknowingly found his creative voice: "The starry sky, the full moon overhead flooding all the landscape with the softest and most beautiful radiance, the white tents covering the hillsides, the large fire blazing fitfully up, surrounded by two hundred or more men who might readily be taken at first glance to be a band of Spanish brigands, all conspired to make a picture that any artist would wish to copy."[33]

Roe was both a brave soldier and an acute observer of his fellow cavalrymen in combat. Within his descriptions of battle action, for example, Roe intersperses the appearance of the terrain as well as the ominous overtones of war, drawing on an extensive vocabulary and excellent attention to detail:

The Third Division of cavalry was encamped on the northwestern edge of the old Bull Run battlefield. The day before we occupied the battlefield itself. The earlier part of the day was spent by two different regiments in preparing to march, and by noon the concentration of the entire command began. Distant outposts, regiments on picket, and scouting parties were drawn in, and soon after the battle-flags of General Kilpatrick, General Davies, and General Custer were seen fluttering through forests or over hills in the direction of the Warrenton and Alexandria pike. Following them were long lines of cavalry and artillery, and above all, a bright October sun that gave to the scene anything but the grimness of war. As evening approached we came out on Warrenton pike. General Davies' brigade had the advance, and part of the Harris Light Cavalry was thrown out as skirmishers. It soon struck the enemy's pickets, and then a running fight was kept up until within a short distance of Gainesville. Our flying artillery took advantage of every high position to send a shell shrieking after the enemy. It was now dark night.[34]

As chaplain, Roe frequently experienced combat: "The early dawn of Saturday morning saw us returning to the battlefield. About nine o'clock we mounted the hill, and formed upon the plain on the opposite side of the river. As we were taking our position, I heard a whizzing sound, and saw the earth torn up by a solid shot quite near me. They soon screamed over our heads and fell all around us. . . ." Among those mortally wounded that day was one of Roe's commanders, General Bayard: "At the hospital we found poor Bayard. Of all the ghastly wounds I saw that day his was the most awful." Roe consoled the general, who had but a few hours to live: "My heart sank within me as he gave me his hand in farewell, and I almost murmured, 'Why are the best taken?' "[35]

As Roe moved throughout the makeshift hospital—a large Southern home now filled with the wounded and dying—he heard "cries and groans" and saw "ghastly and bloody wounds" almost everywhere. Here his realistic depiction of war and its awful consequences demonstrates the observant awareness of a writer/artist, the objective analysis of a soldier, and the anguished feelings of a sympathetic man, helpless to do much more than to offer reassurances and condolences. Roe graphically relates his hospital tour:

Some [soldiers] had their eyes shot out; the tongues of some were swollen out of their mouths; some had their bodies shot through; others were torn and mangled by shell and solid shot, and all were crowded wherever there was any space. The surgeons were hacking off limbs and arms by the dozen. The odor of blood was oppressive. One man called me to him, thinking I was a surgeon, and said that one of his wounds had been dressed, but he found that he had another, which was bleeding rapidly. Another poor fellow held up his arm to me, with a great bulging hole in it, and asked with an expression of pain and anxiety that I could scarcely endure, whether I thought he would have to lose it? Such is the horrid reality of war behind the painted scenes of honor, glory and romance.[36]

Knowing that his regiment probably would be advancing the next day, Roe looked for a place to sleep in the temporary hospital, for "the medical department of our brigade had been rendered small by the absence of some of its members, and it might be that our duties on the morrow would be very arduous. The ground outside the hospital was so tramped up, muddy, and filled with horses, that it was impossible to sleep there. But there was a stone alley-way under the hospital, filled with tobacco in the leaf, part of it lying on the ground, and part drying overhead. One end of this place was already filled with

wounded men, but the surgeon in charge said that the other
would not be occupied before morning, and that I had better
stay there." Again Roe, the minister/chaplain but still a practical
man who usually made an effort to make the best out of the
worst, finally located a small area where he could lie on the
floor and sleep. He inspected the stone alley-way, and "as a
light came I saw something white lying near the wall. I first
thought it was a dog, and going up, I stirred the object with
my foot. On looking closer, I found that it was a ghastly pile
of arms and legs from the amputating-room. But I had seen
so much of blood and horror during the day that I had grown
callous. I quietly spread my blankets within ten feet of the bloody
heap, and listened sadly to the shrieks and groans from the
hospital above till I fell asleep. The reopening of the battle
on Sunday morning awoke me, and as I was rolling up my
blankets, a shell burst near warned me to hasten. I found the
regiment and with it recrossed the [Rappahannock] river."[37]

Like Emerson, who believed one's goodness should have an
edge to it or it is goodness without strength, Roe believed in
being a forceful chaplain: "I often feel it is my duty to be somewhat officious, and to offer my service outside of my regiment
sometimes, for even such as I can give is better than nothing,
which would be their lot if some did not go forward. I think
Christians should be aggressive in their character, and seek op-
portunities to extend the dominion of their King. There are
too many professors [of Christianity] who are like a certain
chaplain, concerning whom I heard an officer remark, 'that he
was a good inoffensive man, and never disturbed the devil nor
any one else in the camp.' "[38]

Frequently included in Chaplain Roe's letters to the New
York *Evangelist* are accounts of Colonel John S. Mosby's guerilla
warfare in northern Virginia, which has sometimes been called
"Mosby's Confederacy." Mosby's raiders, although only about
two hundred men, became notorious to the northern army for
their frequent attacks on supply trains, their destruction of am-
munition dumps and communication lines, along with their rout-
ing of cavalry columns and the now-legendary capture in
February 1861, of a Union general, made prisoner in Fairfax
Courthouse while asleep in his bed. Roe's encounters with Mosby's Marauders were frequent. Note here his use of dialect, a
fictional device he included in almost all of his novels:

The forests and country around us swarm with guerillas. In place of some savage Indian chief, the terror of the whole border, the frontiers of our army are infested by the ubiquitous Mosby. The capture of a sutler's train near Fairfax and a raid upon an outpost on the Rappahannock occurring at the same time are both ascribed to Mosby in person by the soldiers. If a picket hears a distant gallop in the night upon one flank of the army, and a sudden shot startles the air upon the other flank, Mosby is invariably the author of both alarms. No wonder the poor contrabands say, "Mosby mus' be like the debbel and go all ober to oncst!"[39]

But Roe also observed what benefit Mosby's raids had brought about:

This evil has one great advantage, however, and that is the almost entire suppression of straggling. Mosby and his companions have done more to abolish this disgraceful custom in our army than all the orders and edicts from the War Department and Major Generals down. A year or more ago, I saw bodies of men marching in a way that reminded one of a comet, the head of the regiment being the nucleus, the density decreasing rapidly as you went toward the rear, and finally a straggling raft of men scattered over two or three miles constituting the tail. Now you will find a column moving trimly and compactly, and the rear files often looking suspiciously over their shoulders among the dark pines through which they are passing, for sometimes, especially at night, shots are fired into the rear.[40]

Roe concluded his comments on Mosby and his guerillas with his characteristic blending of the practical and the religious, "Thus vigilance is a cardinal virtue in this, as well as in the Christian warfare."

Marriage, Richmond, and Washington

In February 1863, torn between his strong patriotic duty and his desire to be a well-educated minister, Roe resigned his chaplaincy and returned to the Union Theological Seminary of New York to complete his studies. At the end of that school term he decisively resolved his inner conflict: "My regiment would not get another chaplain, so I again returned to it" (*NA*, 483). Thus, he was separated from his troops during the winter of 1862–1863 for approximately one semester. When he returned

to duty his regiment again was doing picket duty, and the struggle had earlier reached a temporary stalemate even for Mosby and his raiders: "The country between the two rivers is now thoroughly occupied by our troops, and our picket lines so close and well posted as to render it almost impossible for the rebels to indulge themselves . . . in many murdering and horse-stealing expeditions."[41]

That same year, in November 1863, Roe received a month's leave of absence from his regiment so that he could be married to Anna Sands. Their marriage was the culmination of a long friendship, courtship, and engagement. Anna's grandfather, Nathaniel Sands, as recalled by Mary Roe was "a 'Friend' and a gentleman in all that the words imply, who was loved and respected by the whole community."[42] Mary Roe has recorded her notes on the marriage: "The ceremony was performed by the venerable Dr. Adams in Madison Square Church [in New York City], and was followed by a large reception at the bride's home in Seventeenth Street, New York. Leaving his bride there when the furlough was over, my brother returned to his regiment."[43]

When Roe returned he found a sincere welcome, particularly the "numberless great brown hands . . . [that] gave me a grip that made my joints snap again [for] it had a language whose meaning I liked. It showed I had the first requisite for doing good among them—their confidence and affection."[44] As Roe recalled, his regiment had set up quarters at Stevensburg, between the town of Culpeper and the Rapidan River. Because the weather was mild and the fighting temporarily quiet, "several of the officers were enjoying the society of their wives. Mrs. Roe having expressed a willingness to rough it with me for a week, I sent for her . . ." (*NA,* 483). One Saturday afternoon Roe went to the nearest railroad station to meet her. The train came but Anna Roe was not on it. The disappointed young bridegroom returned to camp: "I found the return ride of five miles a dreary one in the winter twilight" (*NA,* 483). Stopping at his colonel's tent to inform him (and his wife) that Anna had not been on the train, Roe learned that a dangerous military offensive was being planned: " 'Chaplain,' said the colonel, 'we are going to Richmond to-morrow. We are going to wade right through and past everything in a neck-or-nothing ride, and who will come out is a question.' " Roe could hear the colonel's wife weeping as the colonel reported "that on the morrow General Kilpatrick would lead four thousand picked cavalry-men in a raid on Richmond, having as its special object the release of our prisoners." Roe then rode to General Kilpatrick's headquarters, where the general told him, "You need not go. Noncombatants are not expected to go" (*NA*, 483).

Just before this daring military attack had been planned, Roe had been appointed chaplain of Hampton Hospital, Virginia. President Lincoln had made the appointment, and Roe was now awaiting his confirmation by the United States Senate. As Roe wrote in his memoir, "To go or not to go [on the raid] was a question with me that night. The raid certainly offered a sharp contrast with the anticipated week's outing with my bride. I did not possess by nature that kind of courage which is indifferent to danger, and life had never offered more attractions than at that time. I have since enjoyed Southern hospitality abundantly, and hope to again, but then its prospect was not alluring" (*NA*, 483). Once more Roe's parental examples came through—to face an issue resolutely and make the best moral and ethical decision. "Before morning, however, I reached the decision that I would go, and during the Sunday forenoon held my last service in the regiment. I had disposed of my horse, and so had to take a sorry beast at the last moment, the only one I could obtain" (*NA*, 483–84).

The proposed raid on Richmond was Roe's last combat involvement and also his last Civil War chronicle. He reported both the pains of preparation and the last-minute decision to abort the raid: "On a dreary, drizzling, foggy day we passed a milestone on which was lettered, 'Four miles to Richmond.' It was still 'on to Richmond' with us what seemed a long way farther, and then came a considerable period of hesitancy, in which the command was drawn up for the final dash. The enemy shelled a field near us vigorously, but fortunately, or unfortunately, the fog was so dense that neither party could make accurate observations or do much execution. For reasons that have passed into history, the attack was not made. We withdrew six miles from the city and went into camp" (*NA*, 484). As soon as the raid had been aborted and the troops had settled into camp at Yorktown, General Kilpatrick sent for Roe and gave

him another mission, this time to Washington with special dispatches.

While in Washington, Roe had a brief meeting with President
Lincoln. Roe was impressed by Lincoln, who, "learning that I
had just returned from the raid, sent for me, and I had a memora-
ble interview with him alone in his private room." Roe modestly
in his memoir, as usual, did not mention that news of his sterling
performance as a chaplain and bravery under fire had become
known to the President. In describing the raid on Richmond,
which had been aborted for military reasons, Roe wrote, "I
expressed regret to the President that the object of the raid
had not been accomplished. 'Pick the flint, and try it again,'
said Mr. Lincoln heartily." In his 1888 autobiographical sketch,
Roe concluded his recollection of his interview with Abraham
Lincoln: "I went out from his presence awed by the courage
and sublime simplicity of the man. While he gave the impression
that he was bearing the nation on his heart, one was made to
feel that it was also large enough for sympathy with all striving
with him in the humblest way" (*NA*, 485). Once more, the
future novelist had gathered impressions and experiences that
he would use as he wrote his fiction.

Chaplain for the Wounded

After his meeting with President Lincoln, Roe was joined
by his wife, and they journeyed in March 1864 to the General
Hospital at Hampton, Virginia, near what was then called Fortress Monroe. At first there were few patients in the large
wooden building that was the hospital, but soon the young chaplain had strenuous duties and responsibilities that tested both
his physical and spiritual reserves. When he was with his cavalry
regiment he had gained in vigor and strength, but within two
months at the hospital he lost thirty pounds. Among his numerous responsibilities as hospital chaplain was the conduct of the
funeral services, which particularly affected him: "On one day
I buried as many as twenty-nine men. Every evening, till the
duty became like a nightmare, I followed the dead-cart, filled
up with coffins, once, twice, and often thrice, to the cemetery"
(*NA*, 485–86). Finally, Roe was assigned an associate chaplain,
who relieved him of this heartbreaking task. Looking for what

he called an antidote to his continually depressing daily routine, Roe turned to nature for aid, not only for himself but also for the patients: he transformed a large "waste land" around the hospital into a successful garden, where he and walking convalescents grew vegetables that they turned over to the hospital kitchen by "the wagonload." "If reward were needed," Roe wrote, "the wistful delight with which a patient from the front would regard a raw onion was ample, while for me the care of the homely, growing vegetables and fruits brought a diversion of mind which made life more endurable" (*NA,* 486).

When Roe returned to civilian life he continued his gardening and wrote numerous articles about growing vegetables and fruits, especially strawberries, as well as several horticultural books—*Play and Profit in My Garden* (1873), *Success with Small Fruits* (1888), and *The Home Acre* (published in 1889, after his death). If Roe had wished, it appears that he could have made a successful and profitable career in what he called his gardening, for he became nationally and internationally known for his expertise. Another book, *Driven Back to Eden* (1885), often called a children's book, concerns not only the various aspects of nature—birds, flowers, weather conditions—but also gives information about the best planting and harvesting times for various crops and explores certain aspects of plant growth and production.

While Roe was at Hampton Hospital he became disturbed about the patients' welfare in another way, once more demonstrating the influence of his mother. He was concerned about their reading material, what he called "rations for their minds." In a letter to the *Evangelist* for July 1864, Roe wrote about the patients and their wounds: "I could take you through our wards, and show you long rows of men with thigh amputations, fractured thighs; men who have lost arms, hands, and both their feet; and in short, men with great gaping, ghastly wounds in every part of their body. With such injuries nothing will sustain but cheerful courage; despondency is almost always fatal. The only true basis of such courage is God's religion, but to this all-important condition much can be added that is most excellent."[45] He appealed to the readers of the *Evangelist* to send him books for patients. Already, he wrote, he had a "fair collection" for a religious library, thanks to "some effort, and the kindness of friends." He said that "the Messrs. Harpers, and Appletons, and other prominent city publishers, have generously offered me their books at half price for hospital purposes." But the patients, he said, also needed other books: "The works of Irving, John S. C. Abbott, Dickens, Cooper, Scott and T. S. Arthur, would be invaluable from both a sanitary and a moral point of view, for they would remove the parent of all evils—idleness. Poetry also is very much asked for. My simple request, therefore, is that out of gratitude to the brave suffering men who throng the wards of Hampton Hospital, you would send them good cheerful books."[46] Roe's book project received strong support; he added three thousand volumes to the hospital library.

Among his lasting contributions to Hampton Hospital were his successful efforts to build a new chapel. Taking a short leave of absence, he raised most of the money needed. Again, as he wrote, he made good use of convalescent patients who wished to do physical work: "Northern generosity, and, in the main, convalescent labor, enabled me to build a large, commodious chapel" (NA, 486). Years later, Roe returned for a visit to Hampton Hospital and found the chapel still being used, as was the hospital library.

When the war ended on 9 April 1865, Roe was still at Hampton Hospital. While there he and his wife had contributed a great deal to the physical welfare and spiritual well-being of the patients—religious services, the large vegetable farm (and a little later, even a poultry yard), and the formation of an excellent library and the building of the chapel. By October 1865, Roe's work at the hospital was finished, for it was almost empty. He resigned his chaplaincy in the Union Army, and the early years of Edward Payson Roe—as chaplain/minister and apprentice writer—were completed.

Roe's Creed and Writing Apprenticeship

While conducting his library fund-raising for Hampton Hospital, Roe had written to William H. Wickham, a broker and later mayor of New York City, thanking him for his donation of $100 for the library. In this letter Roe had included the covenant of the Hampton Union Church. This covenant, often referred to as "Roe's Creed," gives an excellent insight into Roe's practical views on religious practices:

Article I—God being my helper, I will try to the best of my ability to be a Christian.

Article II—I will take the word of God for my guide, and trust in Christ alone for salvation.

Article III—I solemnly pledge myself to abstain from profane language; from alcoholic drinks as a beverage, and all other vices in the Army and Camp, and will be a true soldier of my Country and Cross.

Article IV—I will strive earnestly to win souls to Christ, and I will faithfully try to watch over my Christian Brother.

About this creed Roe wrote in the letter to Wickham, "You perceive that it is not very narrow or sectarian," and "since the first of January, 1865, nearly one hundred have lived up to it while they remain in the service."[47]

Besides formulating and espousing a practical religion while he was chaplain, one that could be put into use for everyday life, Roe almost without realizing it was putting together a creative philosophy about writing. He expanded on that philosophy in an essay for the Chicago *Forum,* April 1888, entitled "The Element of Life in Fiction": "With few exceptions, the value of a novel consists in its power to interest," for "through the entire gamut of human experience, whether attuned to the thunder of cannon or to the laughter of children, it is the actual, the real, which lays the strongest and most lasting hold on the attention. I do not mean the hard, superficial realism of the photograph, but that which presents the complete man, woman, or child, soul as well as body, motives as well as manner, the pulsations of the heart rather than the conventionalities impressed by the time and environment. The live novel can be written as long as there are live people to read and feel."[48]

Certain aspects of Roe's capacity to write "live novels" can be discerned during his Civil War chaplaincy. His vivid, realistic on-the-scene accounts of combat and his lamentations for the widespread pain and sorrow on the battlefield and in the hospital indicate Roe's inherent novelistic style and often his subject matter, for within all of his fiction is a combination of "heaven

and earth" (as he called it), with God offering the principal
guiding direction and Christ presenting the ideal life to follow.
In "The Element of Life in Fiction" Roe wrote, "Deep, personal experience, the knowledge that he is no better nor stronger
than others, often brings the writer into close sympathy with
his characters, their successes and failures, their joys, sorrows
and sins. It is difficult to give the ring of truth, the color of
life, to the portrayal of anything remote from the author's knowledge." For Roe, "It is the element of life which gives a novel
this [strong] grasp on the attention of the average reader."⁴⁹

Roe's Civil War chronicles and letters exemplify "the ring
of truth, the color of life" that grasped "the attention of the
average reader." It is these qualities of writing that advanced
Roe so quickly, almost miraculously to the peaks of best-seller-
dom from 1872 to 1900 and beyond. What Fred Lewis Pattee
wrote in 1896 is the most accurate and perceptive understanding
of the reasons for Roe's tremendous success as a popular author.
"Roe is the novelist of the great middle class which constitutes
the reading majority. His novels are singularly fitted to appeal
to the class for which they were written. Their author was a
clergyman who wrote his books with a moral, almost a religious
purpose, a fact that disarmed the suspicious; he dealt with domestic scenes and with characters in humble life, and he mingled
sentiment and sensation with a judicious hand."⁵⁰ What Pattee
also wrote about Roe can apply to both his Civil War writings
and his fiction: "Surely it must be admitted that few novels of
the period [when Roe wrote] have shown more vitality."⁵¹

The vitality of writing, the ring of truth, the color of life,
the fortuitous mingling of sentiment and sensation, the moral
purpose, the appeal to the great middle class—all these elements
were molded in the apprenticeship of Roe's Civil War writings.
They form the basis and strength of his novels.

Chapter Two

Barriers Burned Away:
Prelude and Culmination

Immediately upon his return to civilian life Roe took a short vacation, from October 1865, to January 1866, and at the same time did what he called "candidating for a church," finally choosing a small parish about a mile from West Point at Highland Falls, New York, where, as he wrote, "My wife and I spent nine very happy years" (*NA,* 487). Once more Roe became active in fund-raising for a new church; and just as he did at the Union army hospital in Hampton, Virginia, he started a home garden. Using a small plot at first, he eventually expanded it to three acres.

As soon as he gave his first sermon at Highland Falls he decided that his parishioners and he needed a new church. With characteristic vigor he solicited contributions from personal friends and New York City churches, and he presented lectures on his experiences in the Civil War, very similar to the war chronicles already considered. He traveled many miles to lecture and did well as both a speaker and a fund-raiser. Public lectures were popular then, and Roe capitalized on the interest of audiences in his battlefield adventures. A Providence, Rhode Island, newspaper reported how favorably the fund-raising minister was received: "The Rev. E. P. Roe, of West Point, lectured last night before a fair audience, at Harrington's Opera House, under the auspices of Prescott Post No. 1, G.A.R., on 'Secret Service at the Front; or Scouting and Guerillas.' During the war, said the speaker, the northern people regarded guerillas as irresponsible bands of outlaws, living by violence and plunder."[1] Using his Civil War experience, Roe presented these public lectures (including one on "The Romance of Cavalry Life"), sometimes forty to fifty lectures a year. The new church was built in 1868, but Roe continued on the lecture circuit

until 1872 in order to pay off a $20,000 debt outstanding on
the construction. Just as he had done earlier with his battlefield
reports, Roe was once more unknowingly preparing himself
for his future career as a writer. During his lectures he could
see immediately how effective he was as a speaker, but even
more pertinently as a storyteller.

On 16 September 1868, even though more money was then
still needed to pay for the new church, the cornerstone was
laid. As usual, with his customary modesty and self-depreciation,
Roe would not permit his name to appear on the cornerstone,
and only a Bible was placed inside. But in 1888, after his death,
parishioners placed a plaque in the church vestibule in memory
of their former minister. Today church members can still read
this tribute:

> In Memoriam
> Rev. Edward Payson Roe
> Minister of the
> First Presbyterian Ch. of the Highlands
> 1866–1875
> Author, Pastor, Friend
> This Building Stands the Monument of
> His Earnest Labors.
> Erected: 1868

The Chicago Fire: Creative Inspiration

In October 1871 Roe was preaching, as he has written, "for
a far up-town congregation in New York, with the possibility
of a settlement in view. On Monday following the services of
the Sabbath, the officers of the church were kind enough to
ask me to spend a week with them and visit among the people."
On the same night that Roe was speaking in New York City
and planning to consider the offer of a new ministerial post,
the famous Chicago fire had begun: "the [Monday] morning
papers laid before us the startling fact that the city of Chicago
was burning and that its population was becoming homeless.
The tidings impressed me powerfully, waking the deepest sympathy." Roe at that moment felt some of the same emotions
he had experienced as a chaplain. He wrote, "Here is a phase

of life as remarkable as any witnessed during the war." Obeying an impulse that he could not explain to himself or to his surprised church friends (who wanted him to be their new pastor), Roe informed them he planned to leave at once in order to be "on the scene [in Chicago] as soon as possible" (*NA,* 487).

His comments concerning his overpowering feelings at this time indicate that he was driven by a force he could not control, "for soon [he] was among the smoking ruins [in Chicago], finding an abiding-place with throngs of others in a partially-finished hotel" (*NA,* 487). As he wrote later, "one idea had gained the mastery" of his mind. "I had no clear purpose, no definite plan, beyond that of seeing humanity at a time when it appealed so powerfully to one's sympathy and interest."[2]

Almost beyond his rational comprehension, Roe was thinking creatively. "I hoped eventually to write about the scenes witnessed; but what or how I should write I did not know, nor was I by any means certain that I could produce anything that people would care to read. In brief, my feelings were profoundly moved, and I simply obeyed an impulse to go and see what would come out of it. The ruins were still smoking when I arrived, and every hour deepened the impressions of the great disaster." What happened to Roe during the time he was in Chicago was of seminal significance to him, for it altered his future: "I spent several days, and parts of the nights also, picking my way through the *debris* encumbering the streets, while trying to reproduce in imagination the scenes and events of the awful conflagration.—In this effort I was aided by conversations with all classes of people; and many strange and thrilling experiences were related to me." As usual, Roe sympathetically saw the displaced people and how they were reacting to the sudden destruction of their homes, their businesses, their dreams, along with the deaths and injuries to their families and other loved ones. "Far more interesting than the ruins, however, were the brave citizens already engaged in removing them that they might build anew and better than before. On no battlefield has greater courage been displayed than was shown by the plain business men who then faced their immense misfortune. With shop, factory, and home in ashes, they were still rich in their undaunted courage" (*FN,* 328).

Once more Roe's experiences brought forth previously unre-

alized talents. Witnessing the havoc throughout Chicago, he
wrote, "The very air was electrical. Men sheltered in tents and
board shanties were felt to be men, and they stimulated one
even by the expression of their eyes before they spoke" (*FN*,
328). The great sympathy Roe felt for the homeless, sick, injured, and dead affected him deeply. "For days and nights I
wandered where a city had been, and among the extemporized
places of refuge harboring all classes of people" (*NA*, 487).
In looking back at these experiences, Roe in 1887 was puzzled
as to when this creative surge took place. "I do not remember
just how or when it was, but during those few days of my
visit, the story which resulted began to take a shadowy outline
in my mind. On one night especially, such creative power as
I possessed was awakened" (*FN*, 328). He looked at the area
where he was walking, and his heart overflowed with sorrow
for those harmed by the fire: "There was not an evidence of
life where had been populous streets" (*NA*, 487). Roe's inherent capacities as a boy and young man to combine drama, excitement, and emotions in his narratives—as seen in his stories told
to his sister Mary and other playmates, his chaplain's chronicles
for the New York *Evangelist*, and his lectures to raise money
for a new church at Highland Falls—all these concatenated as
he meditatively walked the streets of Chicago, observing the
effects of the fire on the city and its populace.

One night, as he came to a street where a large beautiful
church had been, he watched the full moon through the roofless
walls and the shattered marble spire. How long he sat there
Roe did not remember, but he believed that "the story had
its beginning on that spot if in any definite place; but all was
still vague and uncertain" (*FN*, 328). He evidently sat for a
long time on the steps of the ruined church, that of the famous
clergyman, Robert Collyer, author of *From Anvil to Pulpit* and
an outstanding leader in bringing relief and reconstruction to
fire-scarred Chicago. The Reverend Collyer's church meant a
great deal to Roe because Collyer, originally trained as a blacksmith in England, came to America, first to Philadelphia, then
Chicago, then New York City, always encouraging the kind
of church Roe praised in his life and later in his fiction, a church
where people of all social classes were represented in the congregation. On these church steps came the general plot of his first

novel. "It was there and then, as nearly as I can remember, that the vague outlines of my first story, 'Barriers Burned Away,' began to take form in my mind." Concluding his Chicago memories, he wrote, "I soon returned home, and began to dream and write, giving, during the following year, such hours as could be withdrawn from many other duties to the construction of the story" (*NA*, 487). Roe's journey to Chicago thus ended, and his creative journey—from 1871 until his death in 1888—began.

The Writing of *Barriers Burned Away*

Leaving Chicago, Roe was profoundly depressed by the miles of terrible devastation and the thousands of homeless people that had confronted him. But he was still motivated to begin the story he had conceived at Collyer's fire-ruined church. He returned to his family and parishioners in Highland Falls and resumed his pastoral responsibilities, including efforts to complete the raising of funds for the new church. In spite of these activities he wrote his first novel whenever he could in good conscience take the time from his ministry. He was under the spell of his writing impetus: "The story, such as it is, was not made nor definitely thought out from the beginning. It simply grew, taking possession of my fancy with very little volition on my part" (*FN*, 328).

I wrote when and where I could,—on steamboats, in railway-cars, and at all odd hours of leisure, often with long breaks in the work of composition caused by the pressure of other affairs, again getting up a sort of white-heat from incessantly dwelling upon scenes and incidents that had become real to me. In brief, the story took possession of my mind, and grew as naturally as a plant or weed in my garden. It will thus be obvious that at nearly middle age, and in obedience to an impulse, I was launched as an author. . . . (*NA*, 487–88)

During the winter of 1871–1872, which Roe called one of the happiest of his life, he made progress on his book while writing in a cottage at Eagle Valley, in the upper area of the village of Highland Falls. He was also discouraged at times, for, looking back in 1888, he wrote, "The writing of sermons certainly does not prepare one for the construction of a novel, and to this day certain critics contemptuously dismiss my books as 'preaching.' " Yet at the same time he was experiencing the creative involvement of the writer: "While writing my first story, I rarely thought of the public, the characters and their experiences absorbing me wholly" (*NA*, 488).

Just as he had done as a boy, Roe tried out his story on his sister, and once more she encouraged his narrative talent. "Little cared I for the wild snow-storm as I walked a mile or so to her residence, and when I returned in the evening, honestly and justly criticised, yet encouraged to go on, the sharp cutting crystals were unheeded" (*FN*, 329). Roe also asked critical advice on his manuscript from his good friend, Dr. Lyman Abbott (1878–1939), the champion of a modern and rational outlook on American Christianity, and co-editor with Henry Ward Beecher of the *Christian Union* (later the *Outlook*). In his letter to Abbott, Roe explained his intent while writing *Barriers Burned Away*. Using the salutation, "Dear Brother," Roe wrote in January 1872: "Would it be convenient for you to give me a little time next week to look over part of the manuscript of which I spoke to you? I have tried to give the story an interest entirely independent of the Chicago fire, so that it may not be as ephemeral as . . . if all turned on that event. In this age events however great soon lose their hold on people's attention. I would prefer that nothing should be said of this matter until something comes of it—perhaps nothing ever may."[3]

Accepting the advice of his sister and Abbott, Roe continued with his manuscript until he had eight chapters completed. Ever a practical man in all his activities, he realized that it would be difficult for an unknown and unpublished writer to have his novel accepted by a publisher. "I knew that there were decided advantages, especially for beginners, in having a story appear first as a serial, for it would be a long step toward securing a publisher of the narrative in book form." Once more he thought of the New York *Evangelist* and the editors, H. M. Field and J. H. Dey, from whom he had received "much kindness." "I felt quite sure that they would give my little fragment of a book as favorable consideration as they could conscientiously, and so, on another stormy wintry day, I made known to them my wishes. Dr. Field asked me if I had my manuscript with me." Presenting his eight chapters to the two editors, Roe read all the pages he had with him. "Before me in the grate was a glowing fire, and for a while I was in doubt whether the story would go into that or into their paper" (*FN*, 329). The two editors, in encouragement, asked Roe to leave the manuscript with them, and thus the serial publication began.

Roe's later account of how the eight chapters grew into fifty-two installments once more shows how unexpected—or, even better, serendipitous—events conspired to help him in his authorial efforts. "I had little idea how long the story would be. We all supposed that a few more chapters would finish it, but it grew from week to week and from month to month. Sometimes I would make a 'spurt' in writing, and get well ahead of the journal, and again interruptions and various duties would prevent my touching the work for weeks, and the paper would catch up and be close at my very heels." This method of writing *Barriers Burned Away,* chapter by chapter, continued for months. "The evolution of the story in my mind, and the task of writing out the pages, occupied about a year, and just fifty-two installments appeared in the *Evangelist.* The serial publication was of much assistance in procuring a publisher for this novel in book form, for the story began to attract attention and secure friends" (*FN*, 329). Once more Roe was overly modest in appraising his own value, for as soon as Dodd & Mead announced the pending publication of *Barriers Burned Away* in book form, letters came to the company from readers of the serial installments in the *Evangelist,* which were still in progress, offering to buy the novel as soon as possible in order to find out how the story would end.

In the summer of 1872, as Roe later remembered, Dodd & Mead agreed to publish the novel: "a 12mo edition at one dollar seventy-five cents per volume was issued about the 1st of December. Much to the surprise of others, and more to me than to any one else, the thirteenth thousand was reached by the following March. Of late years the sale of this book has been steadily increasing, and my publishers have already paid royalty on over one hundred and thirty thousand copies, including a cheap edition" (*FN*, 329). Eventually this first novel was to sell over a million copies. One should realize that this book sale was remarkable for the period, especially because advertising then was modest in comparison to today's blitz approach of saturating the media. In spite of little advertising from the publishers, *Barriers Burned Away* sold steadily and then phenomenally, for the most effective of all types of sales campaigns was selling the novel—word-of-mouth, the recommendation of one reader to another that *Barriers Burned Away* was worth buying and reading.

Histories of the Dodd & Mead firm demonstrate how popular *Barriers Burned Away* and other Roe novels—and even the horticultural books—were from 1872 until the turn of the century and for some years past 1900: "One of the first things that happened to the new partnership of Dodd and Mead was one of the biggest things that happened in the publishing world of that era. One day in 1871 a young clergyman came into the office with a manuscript about the recent Chicago fire. He confessed that it had been declined by one or two other publishers, but he still thought it was good. He was right. The novel was *Barriers Burned Away.*" Very soon the publishers realized that the book was going to have an unusual publishing record. "It started off well, but not explosively; 13,000 was the first season's sales which was a big one in those times. Before long, however, it was taking the public by storm, selling something like a million copies in various editions—a *Gone With the Wind* of the 1870s. For E. P. Roe, the author, this was the start of a tremendously successful career [for] he wrote many more novels. . . . He wrote also several non-fiction books, one of which [*Success with Fruits*] became a famous best-seller. . . ." The success of Roe's books is a publishing phenomenon of another kind as well, for they did not have just a one-time sale, but instead grew steadily in popularity. "At one time the American News Company placed an outright order for 350,000 copies of E. P. Roe's books, one of the largest orders of its kind ever given. The total circulation of these works has been between four and five millions."[4]

The official history of Dodd & Mead is also helpful in explaining the background of the record sales caused by Roe's *Barriers Burned Away* and succeeding novels. "The seventies were troublous years. In 1871 the Chicago fire was practically a national disaster, to be followed a year later by another in Boston which was almost as bad. Then came the financial crises of '73 and a depression which lasted almost six years. Young Mr. Dodd and young Mr. Mead buckled down to work in earnest. They had to try new things to survive." Dodd & Mead also experimented with Roe's first novel: The beginning "of a new kind of publishing, the popular copyright reprint, which today has grown into a large business itself. One hundred thousand copies of *Barriers Burned Away* were brought out in the 'Phoenix Edition' and sold to the trade for 21¢. They were resold as the bookseller wished at from 27¢ to 50¢. Classics had been reprinted in cheap editions before but that was the first of the copyrighted books."[5]

Thus Roe's professional writing career began at age thirty-four, and with it, for both him and the company of Dodd & Mead, a highly profitable partnership in publishing that was to last throughout Roe's lifetime.

Barriers: The Story

As Roe walked through the still-smoldering ruins of the Chicago fire, he believed he could write about the tragic scenes and homeless people he saw there. But he was doubtful how to write about the heartbreaking situations he had witnessed, and he lacked confidence that he would be able to write anything that people would want to buy or read. Yet he was certain that his creative abilities had somehow been awakened while he was in Chicago. The novel that Roe then wrote captured the hearts of thousands of America's reading public. George Ripley of the *New York Tribune* wrote that *Barriers Burned Away* ". . . betrays a power of invention and description which is not met with every day in the writers of popular fiction."[6]

It is important to analyze *Barriers Burned Away* in detail and to call attention to elements of Roe's style that also appear in his later fiction. This examination will set points of reference for the other novels. Most of Roe's novels employ similar plots, settings, and acts of God (deus ex machina) to resolve their action and to bring endings based on hope and faith in God. They also have in common conflicts of character based on moral and ethical principles, almost always combined simultaneously with interconnecting religious beliefs—usually presented by Roe as both flexible and practical as long as one follows the guidance of Christ and relies on the efficacy of prayer.

But what kind of a novel is *Barriers Burned Away,* and why
was it bought and read by millions of readers in America, Canada, and England for thirty years and more? Its phenomenal
reception is at first glance difficult to understand, especially if
one evaluates it by current critical approaches to fiction. Clearly
Barriers was an exceptionally popular novel—a religious novel
typical of the period—only much better written than its contemporaries. An advertising blurb about *Barriers* circulated by Dodd
& Mead outlines the story: "Mr. Roe lays a firm hold upon
the reader's attention in the first chapter of the story, and does
not suffer it to flag for a moment to the close. The plot is
constructed with the art of a natural story-teller. It is a story
of Western life, culminating in the Chicago fire, which, with
all else it swept away, burned down the very strong barriers
which wilfulness and adverse circumstances had put in the way
of Dennis with Christine." George Ripley in his review praised
the book's construction: "Although this story is intended as a
contribution to the library of religious fictitious literature, it is
remarkable to how great a degree the religious element is made
subordinate to the interest of the narrative and the development
of the plot. Whether this is due to the conscious purpose of
the writer, or to the natural impulse of his artistic sense, it is
not necessary to decide. At all events, it relieves his work from
the monotony that so often attaches to what are called religious
novels, and converts the perusal of it from a task to a pleasure."
Ripley also pinpointed *Barriers'* theme: "It is the design of the
author to enforce the application of the Christian graces of character to the common practical relations of life, instead of wasting
them in ethereal and unfruitful contemplations, and especially
to inculcate the efficacy of prayer as the most powerful spiritual
aid in the struggles of the soul with the temptations of the
world."[7]

The plot of *Barriers* involves Dennis Fleet, a well-educated,
talented young man, but without money or employment, and
Christine Ludolph, a young woman, also well educated and talented who is rich and highly placed in the Chicago society of
the 1870s. Both are especially skilled in art and music, with
art their principal professional interest. But they are otherwise
greatly different. Christine's lifestyle is diametrically opposed
to Dennis's.

As the novel opens, Christine is living with her father, her French mother having died several years before. Her father has long dreamed of returning to Germany to restore the family's baronial estate to its former grandeur. For Ludolph—and for Christine—the guiding standards in life are power, money, and high social and financial position. The capacity to control people—in essence, to rule them—dominates their vision of life. Ludolph does not believe in God and Christ or any religion, and he considers religion complete superstition. He has become a rich man through the success of his Art Building, where he sells objets d'art and musical instruments. Because of his astute purchases, keen business sense, and genuine knowledge and appreciation of art and music values, Ludolph's company is now an established success, and his Art Building is patronized by the fashionably rich. He has given Christine only the best in education and travel, and luxury is her standard. She too dreams of the day when they will be rich enough so that Ludolph can sell his company and they can move permanently to Germany to live in feudal splendor. Their plans include Christine's marriage to a German nobleman who would be worthy of a woman of aristocratic lineage, great wealth, and considerable cultural accomplishment.

Dennis Fleet has a family background and upbringing that stress inner character and personal principles, not material possessions, titles, wealth, and social position. As *Barriers* begins, Dennis's father is dying. As he lies on his deathbed, Mr. Fleet believes that he has been several times a failure—as school teacher, law student, and finally as struggling farmer. He has also tried his hand at inventions and enterprises that have turned out to be both impractical and ill-conceived. Yet some of Mr. Fleet's efforts might have succeeded if good fortune or luck, it seems, had been with him at the right moment. Now he is dying in his impoverished farmhouse on the prairie in midwinter, and snowstorms are enveloping the shabby homestead. Dennis has been away for three years in college studying to be a lawyer. Because of his father's serious illness and suddenly worsened financial straits, he has had to withdraw from school and is now on his way home, hoping to arrive before his father dies. Dennis is also bringing medicine his mother had asked him to buy.

In the first chapter of *Barriers,* "Love Unknown," referring to God's love, the basic religious pattern of the story is foreshadowed in the lives of the parents. Mrs. Fleet believes in God completely and has faith that He will guide her through prayer; her husband does not believe in God and bitterly refuses to pray. He becomes distraught and despondent, for not only is he concerned about his critical illness, but he is also fearful that Dennis may bring about his own death by struggling to reach home with the medicine. Disturbed and embittered, the father speaks to his wife: " 'If this should happen . . . if my accursed destiny involves him, your staff and hope, in so horrible a fate, what have I to do but curse God and die?' "[8] As her husband curses God, "the poor woman [felt] that her heart would burst with the agony of that moment" (4). The father finally relents in his downgrading of religion when Dennis at last gets through the heavy snowfall and enters the sickroom. During the cold night that follows, the father grows weaker and the mother prays for her husband's soul and future immortality, hoping that he will be able to die at peace with himself and God. Near dawn of the next day the dying man learns that she has been awake throughout the night, as she tells him, "praying that you might see that God loved you—that you might be reconciled to Him" (11).

The father tenderly looks at his wife. "Two great tears gathered in the man's eyes. His lips quivered a moment, then he said, brokenly, 'Surely God must love me, or He would never have given me—a wife—who would watch and pray for me— the long winter night' " (11). She then pleads with him to be reconciled with God before he dies, telling him how God can help all people, and that eternity is "long enough to make up for the ills of our brief troubled life here" on earth (12).

Soon afterwards the elder Fleet tells his wife that in his delirium he had heard her praying for him. In his dream, as he says, "I felt that I ought to pray myself, and I commenced calling out in my heart, 'God be merciful to me—a sinner.' Then while I prayed, I seemed to see my Saviour's face right above your bowed head." To the dying man, God's expression is one of reproach. "Then it seemed that I fell down at His feet and wept bitterly, and as I did so the look of reproach passed away, and only an expression of love and forgiveness remained. A

sudden rush of peace came into my soul. . . ." The father then
speaks to Dennis, "Thanks to your—mother's prayers,—I believe,—I feel sure that I am forgiven" (13). Later, near death,
the father says his final words to his heartbroken son; speaking
in a calm but resolute voice he says goodbye:

"Dennis, I leave you—little else—than debts,—embarrassments, and
the record of many failures. You must do—the best you can. I am
not able to advise you. Only never love this world as I have. It will
disappoint you. And, *whatever happens, never lose faith in the goodness
of God.* This has been my bane. It has poisoned my life here, and
had it not been for this dear wife, it would have been my destruction
hereafter. For long years—only her patient love—has stood between
me and a miserable end. Next to God—I commit her and your little
sisters to your care. Be true to this most sacred trust." (14–15)

Then, at peace with God and with himself and no longer embittered by the failures of his life, the father peacefully whispers,
" 'Forgiven!' Then his eyes closed, and all was still. They thought
he was gone. But as they stood over him in awed, breathless
silence, his lips again moved. Bending down, they heard in
faint, faraway tones, like an echo from the *other side, 'Forgiven!'* "
(16).

This strongly melodramatic religious scene concludes the first
chapter of *Barriers Burned Away.* Within it is the bedrock upon
which the story is built. Similar to Tolstoy's Ivan Ilyich, who
recognizes the value of an inner life only a few hours before
his death, Mr. Fleet makes a final reconciliation with God, and
in his last few hours he finds life can be peaceful because he
at last perceives, through his wife's prayers, that God's concern
for His people is based on love and kindness. Here the future
life of Dennis Fleet is delineated, for Dennis has been given
these charges by his father—to become the head of the Fleet
family, support his mother and two sisters, trust in God and
"never lose faith in the goodness of God," no matter what
misfortune he may encounter. Like the young Hamlet, in the
subsequent struggles to fulfill his endeavors, Dennis hears his
father's exhortations and tries to follow them. Throughout the
novel, when Dennis becomes discouraged, he sometimes tries
to turn his back on what his father said: *"whatever happens, never*

lose faith in the goodness of God." Dennis finds life exceedingly
difficult and unpleasant, but he learns that faith sustains him
in coping with his own self and the often-hostile world.
After Mr. Fleet's funeral and burial, the farm and house are
sold, and Dennis rents a small house for his mother and sisters.
Although Mr. Fleet had left no money, Mrs. Fleet has a small
annuity from her father, a prosperous man who deplored his
daughter's marriage. Dennis decides to go to Chicago and, very
much as his father thought when he was a young man, believes
he will succeed without much difficulty. For Chicago "seemed
an Eldorado, where fortune, and perhaps fame, might soon be
won." To Dennis, "the world was all before him" and soon
"he would not only place the family beyond want, but surround
them with every luxury." Thus Roe presents Dennis's naiveté
and provincialism. Dennis sets off for Chicago with confidence
but not much else: he has only ten dollars in his pockets. He
has much difficulty in finding employment, and soon, like the
young boy Robin in Nathaniel Hawthorne's "My Kinsman, Major Molineux," he encounters the seamy side of life. In a disreputable hotel where he was directed for lodging he is swindled
out of half of his money. He also learns that his incomplete
college education has prepared him inadequately for employment. He also places his established religious principles first,
even before going hungry. When he is offered a menial job
in a barroom he turns it down because he is against drinking.
   While walking through the snow to his Chicago boardinghouse, Dennis remembers his father's thoughts about God when
he was a young man about Dennis's age. "Perhaps father was
right . . . God was against him, and is also against me, his
son. Does He not visit the iniquity of the fathers upon the
children unto the third and fourth generation? Not but that
He will save us at last, if we ask Him, but there seems some
great wrong that must be severely punished here" (42–43).
Down to his last dollar, Dennis encounters a good Samaritan
in alcoholic Bill Cronk, who is "profane and disreputable," but
"had a great, kindly nature." Bill Cronk drinks for many reasons,
as he humorously says, "When I am down in the mouth I take
a drink to 'liven me up, and when I feel good I take a drink
to make me feel better. When I wouldn't take a drink on my
own hook, I meet somebody that I'd ought to drink with. It

is astonishing how many occasions there are to drink, 'specially when a man's travelling, like me" (47). Cronk sympathizes with Dennis and his being, as Cronk says, "so chopfallen." When Dennis tells Cronk of his money problems and job-hunting difficulties, Dennis takes on a self-pitying tone, and Cronk replies, "Leetle disposed to show the white feather though, to-night, ain't yer?" (49). When Dennis almost gets angry, Cronk, the practical man, searches his mind for work for Dennis, finally advising him to go to a hardware store in the morning, buy a big wooden snow shovel and clean snow off the sidewalks for stores: "You can pick up a good many quarters before night, like enough" (50).

Thus Dennis learns from the alcoholic drover Bill Cronk that he must keep up his hope and spirits. Dennis also learns that one must look beyond a character weakness, such as Cronk's love for the bottle, to discover basic goodness. Dennis that night takes a firmer hold on his manhood, fortified by Bill Cronk's practical advice and by a biblical passage he reads before going to bed. The story in the Bible is about Peter and the fishes, with Christ saying, "Launch out into the deep and let down your net for a draught." With this advice, seemingly direct from Jesus, Dennis prays and goes to bed. In the morning he borrows the boardinghouse shovel and cleans the sidewalk there. After being paid for this with both breakfast and some money, Dennis has enough to buy a snow shovel. By noon he has earned $2.50.

Later in the day, when Dennis decides that he has only enough time for one more snow-clearing job before the stores close, he sees that a large structure, the Ludolph Art Building, still has much unshoveled snow on its sidewalks. He hears Ludolph asking one of his employees if the store's handyman, Pat Murphy, had reported to work that day. As Ludolph starts to reenter the store, Dennis immediately asks if he can clean the slippery sidewalk. Ludolph says yes and tells Dennis to report to the store office for payment when he finishes the job. While Dennis cleans snow from the sidewalk, Pat the Irishman appears, drunk, and angry that Dennis is doing his work. While Pat is trying to hit Dennis, a policeman comes upon the scene and chases Pat into the Art Building, where drunken Pat knocks over an expensive marble statue and breaks it. Ludolph sees this melée and fires Pat. Dennis, after receiving 50¢ for his sidewalk work, asks Ludolph if he can have Pat's job of handyman and janitor. Ludolph is puzzled why Dennis, who looks and acts like a gentleman, would apply for a handyman's job. Honest and innocent Dennis tells Ludolph the whole story. Ludolph hires Dennis— $40 a month paid weekly for the first two months and then $60 a month if Dennis's work is satisfactory. Then, because Dennis has told a "straightforward story," Ludolph also offers him a place to sleep in the store. Grateful Dennis is surprised and pleased with what he considers a generous offer, but Ludolph, who is a shrewd man with a dollar, has hired Dennis to be both the store's handyman and night watchman for one salary.

In *Barriers* Roe steadfastly presented the practical principles of Christianity in order to give his readers guidelines for their daily lives. These values appear frequently. For example, the first conversation between Dennis and his new employer ends as a debate about the purposes and values of religion and belief in God. When applying for the handyman's position, Dennis presents Ludolph with a character reference from his family minister. Ludolph glances at the letter with "good-natured contempt," saying, "This is all right . . ., superstition is an excellent thing for some minds." He then quickly sees that Dennis is pained by this comment on superstition and religion:

"There . . . , I did not mean to hurt your feelings, but to the educated in our land these things seem very childish."
"I should serve you none the worse," said Dennis, with quiet dignity, "if I believed that the duty I owed to you I owed also to God."
Mr. Ludolph looked as if a new idea had struck him, smiled, and said: "Most people's religion, as far as my experience has gone, is not of this practical kind. But I believe I can trust you, and your face and story are worth much more to me than this letter." (63–64)

The following Sunday, after attending a neighborhood church, Dennis writes to his mother, "dwelling on the truth he had discovered of God's wish to make this life happy and successful, as well as the life beyond." Dennis ends his letter: "I have learned that if I will *trust Him* and do [my] present

duty thoroughly, He will not forget me" (67). Dennis desires
to be successful and rise in this world, but he wants to achieve
this success under God's direction without compromising his
Christian values.

At the Art Building, Dennis learns the duties of janitor and
general handyman—sweeping, dusting, mopping, even shining
the clerks' shoes. He also learns more than his menial chores,
for he sees how inartistic are the arrangements for the lovely
and valuable paintings and art pieces in the store. Much of
this poor display work has been done by the clerks and their
supervisor, Schwartz, who lack the imagination and initiative
to do more than their assigned duties. Soon Dennis is using
his inherent artistic talent to assist Schwartz in arranging the
paintings and sculpture. Ludolph quickly notices the improvement and recognizes Dennis's value by putting him in charge
of art displays. Because of his daily association with beautiful
paintings and sculpture, Dennis now renews his interest in art.
As a boy he had taken drawing lessons, and in college too he
had spent some time with drawing and coloring, showing "remarkable aptness." "Now the passion awoke with tenfold force,
and he had not been in his place a week before he began to
make sketches of little things that pleased him" (71).

Dennis shortly encounters Christine Ludolph. Their unexpected meeting puts him at a marked disadvantage, for he is
"dusty and begrimed from mopping, [and] feeding the furnace."
He has stopped for a moment before a painting that several
days before had caught his attention and caused him unpleasant
dreams. The picture depicts a skating scene. A young man is
kneeling before a young woman and adjusting her skate. He
is obviously in love with her, and "it was evident that the favor
[of fastening her skate] was too much for him, and that . . .
[his love] made his hands trembling and unskilful." But the
young woman's expression puzzles Dennis. He asks himself,
"What possessed the man to paint such a lovely face and make
its expression only that of scorn, pride and heartless merriment?"
(76). Dennis is behind the painting, cleaning the frame. He
steps out from behind the picture, "when a vision met his gaze
which startled him to that degree that he dropped his brush
and duster upon the floor, and stood transfixed. There before
him, in flesh and blood it seemed, stood the lady of the picture—

the same dress, the same beautiful blond face, and, above all, the same expression. He was made conscious of his absurd position by a suppressed titter from the clerks at the door, and a broad laugh from Mr. Ludolph. The beautiful face turned toward him for a moment, and he felt himself looked over from head to foot." Dennis quickly sees that Christine Ludolph's "laughing, scornful look" is like that of the young woman in the painting (77).

Christine also has observed the generally inartistic appearance throughout the Art Building, and she convinces her father that she can put to good use her knowledge and training in art to bring order and beauty. Like her father, Christine disdains religion and love, and she longs for the day when they can permanently move to Germany. She gives little attention to her American suitors, and her "admirers were unaware that they had a rival in some as yet unknown German nobleman" (98), the still-to-be-found German her father plans for her to marry as soon as he has gathered enough riches. Both Christine and her father use as their guidance in life the remark of August Ludolph's elderly brother, "Make a fortune in America . . . , and come back and restore the ancient wealth and glory of your family" (84).

Roe thus dramatically presents in *Barriers* the great distances—religious, financial, social—that keep Dennis and Christine apart. "Could two human beings be more widely separated,—separated in that which divides more surely than continents and seas?" This theme, of two main characters separated by social and financial differences, with the crucial difference of their beliefs in religion, becomes a familiar one in the Roe novels. Roe comments in *Barriers,* "Thus it would seem that when circumstances brought the threads of these two lives near each other, Dennis's and Christine's, the most impassable barriers rose between them, and that the threads could never be woven together, or the lives blended. She was the daughter of the wealthy, aristocratic Mr. Ludolph; he was her father's porter." Christine is unlike Dennis: "Next to the love of art, pride and worldly ambition were her strongest characteristics," and "she did not even believe in that which in many young hearts is religion's shadow, love and romance, nor did her father take a more worldly and practical view of life than she" (91).

While Christine is busy rearranging the store's displays, Dennis observes her. She ignores him in every way, even though she knows he is willing to help. "The shrewd Yankee youth saw that her pride would not brook even a curious glance. But while he kept at a most respectful distance he felt that there was no such wide gulf between them as she imagined" (96). Dennis sees the dilemma he faces, for he knows that by birth and education Christine and he are equals but that she sees her position and wealth as preventing her from accepting him as an equal.

While Dennis works at his menial job, he is reviving his artistic potential by sketching and studying painting in every free minute. He also feels better about his ability to take care of his mother and sisters, although his mother can tell from his letters that he is experiencing humiliation because his job is beneath his capacities and because the Ludolphs take a superior and unfriendly attitude toward him. In encouragement Mrs. Fleet writes, "I am no prophetess, my son, but from the sure word of God I predict for you much happiness and prosperity for thus cheering and providing for your widowed mother. Mark my words. God has tried you and not found you wanting. He will soon give you better work to do,—work more in keeping with your character and ability" (103).

Ludolph then assigns the arrangement of a store exhibit to a clerk named Berder, who has little artistic taste. In desperation, Berder accepts Dennis's offer to set up the display for him. When Ludolph sees the arrangement he is greatly pleased; he asks Berder to assemble another group of art pieces. Ludolph and Christine watch Berder. His confusion and inartistic efforts make Ludolph suspicious, and Berder finally blurts out, "Vleet, dere, helped me" (107). By questioning, Ludolph learns that Dennis did the arrangement of the display. Challenging Dennis on the spot, Ludolph orders him to rearrange another area; Dennis does so, pleasing Ludolph a great deal. Ludolph acts decisively, firing Berder and promoting Dennis to Berder's position and salary. As this occurs, Dennis observes that Christine looks at him "somewhat kindly, and with a little honest admiration in her face" (108).

When Ludolph asks Dennis if he can recommend someone to take over his handyman and porter duties, Dennis makes a suggestion: "There is a German lad in my [Sunday school] mission class who has interested me very much. His father is really a superior artist, but is throwing himself away with drink, and his mother is engaged in an almost hopeless effort to support the family" (109). Here the subplot of the Bruder family enters *Barriers*. Berthold Bruder is a superior painter who has so dissipated himself with drink that he is almost penniless, and he has apparently lost his capacity to paint. Bruder, his wife, their teen-age son Ernest, three small children, and a baby are close to starvation when Dennis comes to their flat with the job at the Art Building for Ernest. Dennis fortuitously arrives in time to stop Berthold Bruder from selling the last of the paintings done when he was an artistic success. Before the evening is over, Dennis has told Ernest about his job at the Art Building, sent him to buy groceries, and convinced Bruder that his talent is still alive. Later, Dennis asks Bruder if he will give him art lessons for pay, and the agreement is reached. Three nights a week Bruder will teach Dennis painting. Dennis now has "touched on the matter nearest his heart—his own wish to be an artist, [and] his need of instruction." Before leaving, Dennis asks Bruder to listen to a passage from the Bible, and Dennis reads the story of the demoniac of Gadara, who ends up "sitting at the feet of Jesus, clothed and in his right mind." Bruder thanks Dennis for all he has done: "I feel dot your human sympathy and kindness vill be a great help to me, and somehow I dake him as an earnest dot Gott vil be kind to me too" (124).

When Dennis awakes the next morning, he hears Christine in the store singing and playing the piano. When he finally locates her, she has left the piano and is sketching a figure from a large painting. As they talk, Christine asks Dennis why he had found such a close resemblance between her and the young woman in the skating picture. Reluctantly, Dennis replies, "Well, then, since you wish me to speak frankly, it was your expression. As you stood by the picture you unconsciously assumed the look and manner of the painted girl. And all the evening and morning I had been troubling over the picture and wondering how an artist could paint so lovely a face, and make it express only scorn and pride. It seemed to me that such a face ought to have been put to nobler uses" (127). That day Christine and Dennis work together in arranging the displays; Ernest does well at work and pleases Ludolph; and Dennis begins his intensive training under Berthold Bruder, who readily believes Dennis can be a superior artist. During the weeks that follow, as Dennis helps Christine, he falls in love with her, even though he knows she has no sympathy with democratic principles and Christian values. "A true, pure love was growing up within his heart. . . . It seemed as if some strong magician's wand had touched the world or him. Everything was transfigured, and no wonder-land was more full of interest than that in which he existed. His life was a waking dream . . ." (141). Christine, however, continues to consider Dennis as only her father's clerk, a trusted and agreeable servant, thus holding firm to the Ludolph views on nobles and peasants.

Still using him only as a helper, Christine asks Dennis to assist her, as a favor, with a charity entertainment she is supervising: he will be the stage manager of several musical tableaux at a large mansion owned by a rich brewer named Brown. Readily agreeing, Dennis finds that Christine's friends, including Miss Brown in particular, treat him as a servant at the affair, sometimes contemptuously. Before the entertainment begins, Christine talks loudly enough for Dennis to hear her ideas about birth and rank, and later her strong belief that the Bible is obsolete for thinking people. Dennis comforts himself with "a grave, quiet dignity," but Christine realizes what she and her friends have done and she is embarrassed. Yet, soon after, she derides Christ and the symbol of His cross. Dennis finally retaliates. When Christine says, "It [the cross] will never have the power to inspire the heart again, as when the Crusaders—," Dennis acts quickly: "At that moment their eyes were blinded by a sudden, dazzling light. There was a general and startled exclamation, and then, awe-struck and silent, they gazed as if spellbound upon a luminous cross blazing before them." At the same moment, Dennis steps from behind this cross (which is made of metal, and by the use of gas jets appears as if on fire), saying, "I should be false to myself, false to my faith—should I remain silent in view of what I have been compelled to hear. That sacred emblem has not spent its meaning, or its power. Millions to-day would die for the sake of Him who suffered on it." Looking directly at Christine, Dennis says, "Could I be a true man and be silent, believing what I do? Could I hear the name

of my Best Friend thus spoken of, and say not one word in
His behalf?" He states, "I regret more deeply than words can
express that you honestly think as you do. But if I honestly
believe the Bible, am I not acting as you said a true follower
ought? For I assure you it is a heavier cross than you can ever
know to speak thus unbidden where I am regarded only as a
serving-man" (160–62). Christine admits that Dennis is entitled
to his opinion. The men in the entertainment then arrive, and
everyone continues to prepare for the various tableaux. But
Christine learns that the gentleman tenor is not present because
he is sick. His part is an important and large one, and it seems
as though some of the evening's affair will have to be canceled.
Now there is general disappointment that Christine and the
tenor will not be able to present their duet, a high point of
the entertainment. Once more Dennis is willing to help, for
he has been singing almost all his life, it seems, and took several
voice courses while in college. The young women urge Dennis
to try out the music before the guests arrive. All except Christine
and her friend Susie Winthrop hope he will do badly. They
feel sorry that he will soon be humiliated. After some false
starts, caused mainly by poor and deliberately off-key piano
accompaniment, Christine volunteers to play the piano while
Dennis sings. Soon "[his] rich, powerful tenor voice startled
and then entranced them all." The snobbish women look at
him in amazement, and Dennis says, "But no one could join
our musical club at college who could not read anything placed
before him" (166). In a quick rehearsal Dennis then sings all
the music arranged for the missing tenor.

The evening's entertainment is received well by the audience,
and Dennis handles his responsibilities as stage manager with
expert attention. The hit of the evening is the duet sung by
Christine and Dennis; they sing in "perfect harmony," Dennis's
voice being received with much surprise and applause. The audience enthusiastically demands an encore. During this duet, cho-
sen by Christine, Dennis sings a love song from the heart, and
without realizing it himself, expresses his love for Christine.
"Dennis had achieved a greater success than Christine, because,
singing from the heart, he had touched the heart" (174). Later,
while watching the entertainment and Christine, Dennis finally
realizes his true feelings about her; "the knowledge stunned

and bewildered him, and his mind was a confused blur" (176). Shortly after the society entertainment, Ludolph promotes Dennis, relieving him completely of the handyman-porter duties that he had still been doing in order to help young Bruder. Also just after the party, Christine becomes ill, and it appears that she may have smallpox. Because a nurse would be almost impossible to employ due to the disease's contagion, Dennis informs his employer that he believes his mother would volunteer to nurse Christine. "She has had the smallpox and would not be afraid" (198). Ludolph is pleased with this possible arrangement and so is Christine. Even though Christine recovers without contracting smallpox, once more Dennis has been ready to help when needed, this time through his mother.

After some time passes, Ludolph fully recognizes Dennis's value to the Art Building and promotes him to a position where he will soon take over the responsible duties of Schwartz, the general supervisor, who gradually is transferred to bookkeeper. During these passing weeks, too, Berthold Bruder has been making progress as he teaches painting to Dennis, who, it appears, can be an outstanding artist. Dennis's critical knowledge of art also has grown prodigiously, thanks to his studies and the tutelage of Bruder. At the Art Building, during a general confusion between two paintings—a masterpiece and a remarkable copy—Dennis stays in the background when the art experts who have been called in argue over the original and the imitation. Christine involves Dennis in this dispute in an effort to humble him, saying sarcastically, "Perhaps Mr. Fleet from his superior knowledge and long experience can settle this question" (221). Looking at the two paintings side by side, Dennis identifies the imitation as a lifeless copy, saying that the artist lacked dynamic emotions and heartfelt sincerity of feeling. One of the art critics then steps forward, examines the original and the copy—taking his details from Dennis's critique—and declares that Dennis's judgment is correct. Once more circumstances separate Dennis and Christine, for "he met Christine's look of agony and hate, and like lightning it flashed through his mind, 'She painted the picture' " (222).

As a result of this episode, Dennis becomes well known as an art critic and soon receives several offers of employment elsewhere, but he stays at the Art Building. Later, too, when

Dennis and Christine meet, he says, "Your power of imitation is wonderful. *You can copy anything you see*" (246). Christine observes how Dennis's expressive face reflects all of his innermost feelings. "Then like a flash came a suggestion—'You can make him love you, and copy feeling, passion, life—from the *living* face.' " She plans what to do: "Perhaps I can inspire love in him, and then make his face a study" (249). By using her smiles and often looking at Dennis with much pleasure, she causes him to return her encouraging looks: "The poor victim loves me already," she said. "The mischief is done. I have only to avail myself of what exists from no fault of mine, and surely I ought to; otherwise the passion of the infatuated youth will be utterly wasted, and do no one any good" (250). Christine starts her underhanded plan to paint true love as Dennis's face displays it, but without any love, even affection, for Dennis in her own heart. Thus "Dennis and his love were put to use somewhat as a human subject might be if dissected alive" (250).

This plot development of Christine's misuse of Dennis's love dominates a large portion of *Barriers Burned Away*. Christine furthers her interests by asking Dennis to complete the overall artistic arrangements at the Art Building. She also asks her father to invite Dennis to the Ludolph apartment so Dennis can sing the tenor parts in new German music the Ludolphs have just brought home. Then, after convincing her father to buy a large attractive mansion, Christine tells Dennis she needs his help in redecorating the expensive house: "Dennis Fleet was the human victim that she was offering on the altar of her ambition" (273). Christine is relentless in capturing in paint the expression of Dennis's love for her, while concealing from him her lack of sincere reciprocity. In the final day of her surreptitious scheme she deceitfully leads Dennis into telling her of his love. While she encourages him by looks and words to speak his heart, she goes to her painting and paints quickly and expertly (concealing from Dennis what she is doing), as the innocent and sincere beauty of his love radiates from his face and eyes. Christine completes the final strokes just as Dennis speaks his full declaration of love for her. However, before he speaks his fullest emotions, he begins to suspect Christine's intentions, for he sees that she is more interested in her painting than his words. Then he realizes, "It is my face, not myself, that she wants!" In an instant he stands by her side, looking at the painting she had previously kept hidden from him. Pointing at it, Christine exclaims in revenge, "Criticise that, if you can! Deny that there is soul, life, feeling there, if you dare!" Dennis sees "a figure and features suggesting his own, pleading with all the eloquence of true love before the averted face of the maiden in the picture. It was indeed a triumph, having all the power of the reality" (279–80).

In his disillusionment, Dennis whispers, almost to himself, "Ah, my God! How cold she must be when she can see any one look like that, and yet copy the expression as from a painted face upon the wall!" (280). As he looks at the painting, Dennis's pride and indignation rise, and "he seized a brush of paint and drew it over the face that had cost him and Christine so much, and then turned and looked at her, saying, 'You have been false,' and 'You have acted a lie before me for weeks.'" As she protests his destruction of her painting, Dennis says, "A moment since I loved you with a devotion that you will never receive again. But now I despise you. . . . Never dream of success till you are changed utterly. Only the noble in deed and in truth can reach high and noble art." He departs with pity in his voice: "May God forgive you" (280–82).

Goodness wronged has taken direct retaliatory action. Roe apparently remembered how Christ vigorously responded as He threw the money changers out of the temple. The principal characters in Roe's fiction frequently are unusually good people, but they also respond with firmness to injustice and cruelty, unafraid to take matters into their own hands. In *Barriers* Dennis is never afraid to speak out for goodness and God.

After this upsetting scene with Christine, Dennis pursues a more rigorous schedule than he ever has before—learning his new position at the Art Building, taking painting lessons from Bruder, studying art, and painting for long hours at his easel, sometimes until dawn. Christine, on the other hand, tries to restore her painting but now finds she has lost all interest in it.

Shortly after his confrontation with Christine, Dennis becomes seriously ill and is taken home to his mother and sisters. Learning about his illness, Christine takes the opportunity to go to his rooms in the Art Building in order to examine his most recent paintings. As she looks at them intently, she finally realizes how Dennis sees life and living—as an individual's efforts to be good and to be helpful to others. Later, young Ernest Bruder informs her about Dennis, "Fader wrote moder Mr. Fleet was no better. I fear he die" (295). From Susie Winthrop Christine learns that Dennis is not expected to live. Going to the Bruder home, Christine finds that Berthold Bruder is with Mrs. Fleet, helping her to care for Dennis. Through Mrs. Bruder Christine reads a letter from Mr. Bruder who calls her the murderer of Dennis, for Dennis calls out in his delirium for Christine. As she returns to her own home, August Ludolph also reports that Dennis is now very critically ill and will be dead soon.

Roe here has created a strong strand of excellent narrative, as Christine is bombarded from all sources by the seriousness of Dennis's illness and her awareness of how much she has contributed to his physical weakness. She also begins to have some doubts about the dream of going to Germany as her father and she have long wished. Dennis's illness has caused her to question most of her values.

Primarily to please Christine and to help her recover from her part in Dennis's imminent death, her father takes her East, and on their way to New York City they stop near West Point and stay at the Cozzens' Hotel. (Roe had a garden plot in Highland Falls several hundred feet from the Parry House and the Cozzens' Hotel.) During their stay Christine is the center of attention at the evening dinners and dances, as "officers from the post and civilians alike eagerly sought her hand, and hundreds of admiring eyes followed as she swept through the mazes of the dance, the embodiment of grace and beauty. She was very gay, and her repartee was often brilliant, but a close observer would have seen something forced and unnatural in all" (304). Her thoughts of Dennis and his illness still are with her. The Ludolphs take a long buggy ride, while at the hotel, for "never before [for Christine] had this passion for the beautiful in nature been so gratified, and all the artist feeling within her awoke" (305) as she saw the beautiful scenery on all the hills. But, at times, shattering these beautiful scenes, Christine thinks how much Dennis would have appreciated the natural beauty she is seeing; she says to herself, *"He—he is dead!—he must be by this time!"* (307).

When the Ludolphs return to Chicago, Christine is feeling regret and sorrow about the harm she has done Dennis. When she is asked to sing at a large party, and among the songs is the one she and Dennis sang at the charity entertainment, she breaks down publicly, leaving the room in tears. But, unknown to Christine, Dennis has made a miraculous recovery from his illness and, though still very weak, is not dead but alive. August Ludolph learns this from young Ernest Bruder but does not tell Christine. Several months later Dennis, still thin and pale, returns to his position at the Art Building, and he also finds a cottage in the city for his mother and sisters.

Shortly after Mrs. Fleet moves into her new home, where Dennis also lives now, she becomes ill, growing feebler each day because of her age. Her illness gives Dennis and his mother many moments of serious conversation. He tells her that he still loves Christine, and she tells him the marriage would not be a good one because he and Christine would be separated because of their beliefs about God. Dennis asks his mother to pray with him for Christine: "Oh, pray for her,—for my sake as well as hers." Mrs. Fleet here articulates one of the main religious themes in *Barriers*. In talking to Dennis about praying to God for guidance, she states, " 'If He chooses that the dross in her character should be burned away, and your two lives fused, there are in His providence just the fiery trials, just the circumstances that will bring it about." (Was she, Roe interjects, unconsciously uttering a prophecy?) "The crucible of affliction, the test of some great emergency, will often develop a seemingly weak and frivolous girl into noble life, where there is real gold of latent worth to be acted on." Dennis agrees with his mother and speaks favorably about Christine: "Her character is strong, and I think most decided in its present bent. But as you say, if the Divine Alchemist wills it, He can change even the dross to gold, and turn unbelief to faith" (329–30). In this way Roe foreshadows the climax, for so far the conflict between Dennis and Christine seems to be irreconcilable. The barriers are high and almost insurmountable—social and financial positions, attitudes toward other people no matter their status in life, and, most crucially, their divergent views about God and what He means to Dennis (and to Roe)—goodness, love, hope, and faith.

Almost six months after Dennis destroyed Christine's painting of his love for her, and after weeks of lethargic interest in her life, Christine comes to the Art Building, still unaware that Dennis is alive or that Dennis's mother is critically ill. Her father has not told her about Dennis's return to work because she has refused to discuss Dennis with him. At her father's urging she reluctantly comes to the Art Building to see a newly arrived painting, bringing her sketchbook with her. While she is sketching, Dennis comes upon her. The shock of this face-to-face encounter is almost too much for each of them. She is astonished and puzzled, he overwrought and then angry. When Christine sees Dennis carrying a painting into the room, her reaction is one of bewilderment: "Her sketching materials fell clattering to the floor, and after one sharp exclamation of alarm she stood as if transfixed, with parted lips and dilated eyes, panting like a frightened bird." Dennis believes she is still bitter about their last disagreement, and he says, "You need not shrink as if from contagion. We can treat each other as courteous strangers." She replies, "I—I—I—thought you were dead!" With anger and indignation Dennis sternly speaks, "What! . . . do you mean to say that you never cared even to ask whether I lived or died in my long, weary illness?—that you were so supremely indifferent to my fate that you could not articulate one sentence of inquiry? Surely this is the very sublimity of heartlessness; this is to be callous beyond one's power of imagination." As Christine eagerly tries to reply, Dennis shouts at her, "You thought I was dead! The wish probably was father to the thought." He hurries away, saying, "But permit me to tell you, though all unbidden, I did not die. With God's blessing I expect to live to a good old age, and intend that but few years shall pass before my name is as well known and honored as the ancient one of Ludolph."

Among the words Dennis says in his anger, Christine remembers most what he says about his love for her: "But after all the wealth of affection that I lavished upon you, after toiling and almost dying in my vain effort to touch your marble heart, you have not even the humanity to ask if I am above ground!" (332–334) As Christine reflects on this traumatic episode, she sees how foolish and inconsiderate she has been with her social position and imagined superiority. She now believes that Dennis despises her, and she can see why. She had only to inquire about his health, but she never did so because of her Ludolph pride. Timidly, almost frighteningly, she now sees herself as Dennis sees her and as he hoped she would. The revelation causes her to speak aloud, in a faint whisper, "I fear—I almost fear I love him" (337).

In desperation that night she tells her father what has happened between her and Dennis—how she abused his love with her painting, how she failed to inquire about his health, their chance meeting in the Art Building. Instead of being sympathetic, August Ludolph praises her for her efforts to utilize Dennis's love for her artistic purposes, and he laughs aloud at her belief that she caused at least some of Dennis's sickness. To Ludolph, Christine's experiment with Dennis and her painting failed because she was too tenderhearted. As they part that evening, Christine still is perplexed about her relationship with Dennis, but her father, speaking to himself, is resolute: "This Fleet is a most dangerous fellow. I wish I were well rid of him. . . . But I had better keep him in my employ during the few months we still remain in this land, as I can watch over him, and guard against his influence better than if he were beyond my control. But no more promotion or encouragement does he get from me" (342). To help him in his surveillance, Ludolph bribes Christine's French maid to spy upon her mistress and report on any meetings or messages involving Dennis. In her room, Christine decides not to tell her father anything further about Dennis, but she also begins to prepare herself for the permanent move to Germany.

Within a short time Christine learns of Mrs. Fleet's illness and anonymously sends her flowers and fruit. In talking with Dennis once more about Christine, Mrs. Fleet decides to send a note with Mrs. Bruder to Christine: "Would Miss Ludolph be willing to come and see a dying woman?/ETHEL FLEET" (350). The note is intercepted by Christine's maid, who also stops the sending of the flowers and the fruit by not delivering Christine's notes ordering them. The maid gives Ludolph Mrs. Fleet's note, and he burns it. When Christine does not come to see his dying mother, once more Dennis becomes angry and bitter. When his mother is dying, she whispers to Dennis, "Pray for *her*. I don't know—why—she seems very—near to me" (353).

When Dennis returns to the Art Building after burying his
mother and finding a home for his two little sisters with an
aunt, Ernest Bruder gives Dennis a note from August Ludolph,
a note with a "small balance" due Dennis: he has dismissed
Dennis from his job. Dennis decides to become a full-time artist.
First, though, he helps Ernest Bruder locate another job, and
he aids the Bruder family when Berthold Bruder—greatly weak-
ened, as Roe emphasizes, by excessive drinking—dies of typhoid
fever. Dennis also decides to enter a Chicago-wide art competition, hoping to gain both the $2,000 first prize and his reputation
as an artist. Working almost as a recluse, he spends many hours
over his painting. Christine, still thinking about Dennis, goes
to the Art Building to see him, but she learns that he has been
dismissed. Confronting her father, she upbraids him for what
he has done. In reply, Ludolph says that his family has always
handled their matters "arbitrarily." In delight, he also tells Christine, "I have received letters announcing the death of my brother
and his wife. I am now Baron Ludolph!" (363). Christine is
greatly distraught about Dennis and, much to her own surprise,
not pleased about the news from Germany and their imminent
departure.

After Christine hears about her father's most recent plans
to return to Germany as quickly as possible to restore the family's
estate and castle, and to begin his long-awaited life as Baron
Ludolph with Christine as Baroness Ludolph, she has only a
short time to reflect on her growing love for Dennis Fleet.
Because she has learned that Dennis has entered Chicago's art
contest, she too decides to enter, hoping that through her painting she can convey to him her message of true love. The day
of the Chicago Art Exhibition soon arrives. All the paintings
on exhibit are anonymous, with the artists' names in sealed
envelopes on the backs of the frames. Dennis has entered a
painting with two scenes, one of a young woman symbolically
a prisoner of the master of a large chateau, the second of a
young woman helping her lover as they climb up a mountain,
with "her pure, noble face . . . lifted up toward *him* . . . ,
and [with] an eager, happy light [that] shone from her eyes."
Nature is an integral part, with trees, rocks, the sky, hills, and
mountains forming a beautiful backdrop to the "emblematic
pictures" (371, 369). Christine at once recognizes Dennis's

painting and understands its message. Christine's entry depicts a young woman on a lonely shore watching a ship sail away from her. "Though every part had been worked up with exquisite finish, the whole force and power of the painting lay in the expression of the woman's face, which was an indescribable mingling of longing and despair" (372). Dennis is certain this is Christine's painting, but she has tried to keep it a secret, not even putting her name in an envelope. The judges award Dennis's painting first prize and "the smaller painting" (Christine's) second. When Christine offers her congratulations to Dennis he responds coldly, thinking of how (he still believes) she failed to respond to his mother's deathbed request. The $2,000 check means little to him because he thinks that Christine and he have irreconcilable differences that will always keep them separated. He has learned too that Christine and her father will soon sail for Europe. When Dennis goes to church the next morning to teach his Sunday school class, he thinks about her, hoping that there can be some way for them to reach an understanding:

He cried unto the Lord for strength and help, and almost lost consciousness of the service in his earnest prayer for true manhood and courage to go forward to what he feared would be a sad and lonely life. And the answer came; for a sense of power and readiness to do God's will, and withal a strange hopefulness, inspired him. Trusting in the Divine strength, he felt that he could meet his future now, whatever it might be. (379)

As Dennis leaves the church he hears fire-alarm bells, and recalls that he also heard them before going to sleep the night before. "Again the alarm-bells were ringing, and there was a light in the southwest" (379), the section of Chicago in which Mrs. Bruder and her children live. Becoming concerned about them, he quickly hurries to the fire. It already is much larger than he expected, and dangerously close to the Bruders' second-floor flat. Dennis sees at once that only immediate action will save them. He alerts Mrs. Bruder and helps her rescue the small children, leading them all to a safe place. Suddenly Mrs. Bruder remembers her husband's most treasured painting: "Dot picture saved mine Berthold life—yes, more, more, him brought

back his artist soul. Vithout him ve vould all be vorse dan dead.
I can no live vidout him." She rushes back into the building,
which is now fully ablaze, before she can be stopped. When
she reached the beautiful painting, "She tore it from its fasten-
ings, pressed her lips fervently against it, regained the street,
but with dress on fire. She staggered forward a few steps in
the hot stifling air and smoke, and then fell upon her burden.
Spreading her arms over it, to protect it even in death, the
mother's heart went out in agony toward her children. 'Ah
merciful Gott! take care of dem,' she sighed, and the prayer
and the spirit that breathed it went up to heaven together"
(382).

After taking care of the Bruder children, and temporarily
entrusting them to young Ernest, Dennis helps women and children to escape from the blazing neighborhood. Dennis realizes
he has to get back to his own room: "His two thousand dollars
and all his possessions were there, and the instinct of self-preser-
vation caused him to think it was time to look after his own.
But progress was now very difficult. The streets were choked
by drays, carriages, furniture, trunks, and every degree and
condition of humanity." As Dennis rushes ahead he hears a
woman screaming in fright from the third-story window of a
burning mansion. "Who will volunteer with me to save that
woman?" he shouts. An answer comes back at once: "Wal,
stranger, you can reckon on this old stager for one," answered
a familiar voice. Dennis turned and recognized his old friend,
the Good Samaritan. "Why, Cronk," he cried, "don't you know
me? Don't you remember the young man you saved from
starving by suggesting the snow-shovel business?" Exchang-
ing sincere greetings as they look for a ladder and rope,
Dennis and Bill Cronk work rapidly to save the young
woman, who turns out to be Miss Brown, one of the socialites
who were rude to Dennis at the charity entertainment. By a
feat of acrobatic skill Dennis uses the ladder and rope to get
to the young woman, then lowers her by the same rope to
Cronk, who catches her where he is waiting at the top of the
ladder.

When she is safe, Miss Brown, the daughter of a rich brewer,
recognizes Dennis.

"Is not this Mr. Fleet?" asked Miss Brown.
"Yes."
"How can we ever repay you?"
"By learning to respect honest men, even though they are not rich, Miss Brown."
"Did you know who it was when you saved me?"
"Yes."
"Mr. Fleet, I sincerely ask your pardon."
But before Dennis could reply they were compelled to fly for their lives. (385–87)

Throughout these fire scenes Roe intersperses his own first-hand observations of Chicago in 1871. These descriptions are excellent, and Roe's imagination was clearly at its zenith as he dramatically wrote about the fire's destructive forces after seeing only the smoking ruins: "The rush and roar of the winds and flames were like the thunder of Niagara, and to this awful mono-tone accompaniment was added a Babel of sounds—shrieks, and shouts of human voices, the sharp crash of falling buildings, and ever and anon heavy detonations, as the fire reached explo-sive material" (389).

Comprehending at last the awesome destruction of the fire, Dennis runs toward his room to try to save whatever he can. Hurrying by the Art Building, he sees a man rush past him and put a passkey in the side door. Dennis shouts, "Mr. Ludolph, it is not safe to enter," but August Ludolph ignores Dennis's cry and turns on him with anger, "his face . . . black with passion and distorted with rage." Dennis cries out again for Ludolph to come back. Ludolph replies, "I will get certain pa-pers, though the heavens fall!" finishing his retort to Dennis "with an oath." Dennis, hearing "an awful rushing sound in the air" and dodging the "hot bricks [that] rained around him," runs for cover.

When he turned to look, the Art Building was a crushed and blazing ruin. Sweet girlish faces that had smiled upon him from the walls, beautiful classical faces that had inspired his artist soul, stern Roman faces, that had made the past seem real, the human faces of gods and goddesses that made mythology seem not wholly a myth, and the white marble faces of the statuary, that ever reminded him of

Christine, were now all blackened and defaced forever. But not of these he thought, as he shudderingly covered his eyes to shut out the vision; but of that terrible face that in the darkness had yelled defiance to heaven. (390)

Stunned by what he had seen, Dennis stumbles along toward his room when he hears a shout—"The north side is burning!" (391). Quickly remembering Christine and her safety, he has to struggle through the milling mobs to reach the Ludolph mansion. The thought of Christine gives Dennis almost superhuman power to push forward. Finding the doors and lower windows of the mansion locked and protected, Dennis sees that he might enter by breaking a window on the balcony outside of Christine's second-floor art studio. Climbing a nearby elm tree Dennis jumps down to the balcony, breaks a window, and enters the silent and dark studio: "What a rush of memories came over him as he looked around the familiar place! There was the spot on which he had stood and asked for the love that he had valued more than life. There stood the easel on which, through Christine's gifted touch, his painted face had pleaded with scarcely less eloquence, till he blotted it out with his own hand. In memory of it all his heart again failed him, and he sighed, 'She will never love me.' But there was no time for sentiment" (393).

Searching in the dark, he finds Christine's bedroom, where she lies sleeping soundly under the influence of medication. Although he at last awakens her, she believes, in her drugged condition, that he is not Dennis Fleet. He quickly pulls open the bedroom drapes, opens the shutters, "and the fire filled the room with the glare of noonday. At that moment an explosion occurred which shook the very earth" (396). Frightened and bewildered, Christine is unable to dress herself. "Dennis saw that in the terrible emergency he must act the part of a brother or husband, and springing forward he assisted her with the dexterity he learned in childhood" (399). He then wraps her in a blanket shawl, and, with walls crashing and roofs falling about them, they run for safety.

In a chapter entitled "On the Beach" Roe describes the fire's great intensity and awful destruction, and Dennis's superhuman efforts to carry the unconscious Christine to the protection of the lake. Throwing her into the back of a runaway express wagon and covering her face, he "crouched beside her, trusting all now to God" as the "horses rushed madly on till they plunged into the lake. At the sound of water Dennis lifted his head and gave a cry of joy. It seemed that the hand of God had snatched them from death" (404). When morning comes, Christine and Dennis look around them.

> The sun had now risen quite above the waters of the lake, but seen through the lurid smoke which swept over its face, it seemed like one of the great red cinders that were continually sailing over their heads. In the frightful glare, the transition from night to day had scarcely been noted. The long, narrow beach was occupied by thousands of fugitives, who were hemmed in on every side. On the south was the river, skirted with fire, while opposite, on the west, the heat was almost intolerable; on the east were the cold waves of the lake, and on the north a burning pier that they could not cross. Their only hope was to cling to that narrow line where fire and water mingled, and with one element to fight the other. (407)

Danger is all around them. "Upon this heterogeneous mass of humanity the fire rained down almost as we imagine it to have fallen upon the doomed cities of the plain, and the hot breath of the flames scorched the exposed cheek and crisped even eyebrows and hair. Sparks, flakes, cinders, pieces of roof, and fiery pebbles seemed to fill the air, and often cries and shrieks announced that furniture and bedding which had been dragged thither, and even the clothing of women and children, were burning." The beach is not only crowded with the people, their possessions, but also with many animals. "Added to all the other terrors of the scene was the presence of large numbers of horses and cattle, snorting and plunging in their fright and pain." All this Dennis sympathetically observes, helping whenever he can. "But the sound that smote Dennis's heart with the deepest commiseration was the continuous wail of helpless little children, many of them utterly separated from parents and friends, and in the very agony of fear" (408).

As the day advances, and the flames become hotter and closer, the people on the beach must finally enter the water for safety. Plunging into the breakers with Christine, Dennis keeps her from harm, saying, "Courage. . . . With God's help I will save

you yet." As Christine looks at his kind face, "a great and generous impulse, the richest, ripest fruit of her human love, throbbed
at her heart, and faltered from her lips—'. . . I am not worthy
of this risk on your part. If you will leave me you can save
your own life, and your life is worth so much more than mine!' "
(410). During an hour of "extreme danger," the two of them
struggle to keep from drowning in the waves of the lake:

> Standing with the cold billows of the lake breaking round him,
> and the billows of fire still rolling overhead, Dennis began to sing
> in his loud, clear voice:—

> > "Jesus, lover of my soul,
> > Let me to Thy bosom fly,
> > While the billows near me roll,
> > While the tempest still is high."

> Voice after voice joined in, some loud and strong, but others weak
> and trembling—the pitiful cry of poor terror-stricken women to the
> only One who it seemed could help them in their bitter extremity.
> Never before were those beautiful words sung in such accents of
> clinging, touching faith. Its sweet cadence was heard above the roar
> of the flames and breakers. (411)

Dennis's singing strengthens the spiritual courage of all those
for miles around on the beach. He frequently reassures Christine
by telling her that he is relying on God's guidance and that
God's love has given him the needed strength and desire to
help others. Christine remains skeptical and puzzled about God
until Dennis is hurt while protecting a young woman from being
robbed and abused by a drunken man. As she brings Dennis
back to consciousness, she asks him how God could permit
"wrong" (the drunken robber) to triumph over "right" (Dennis). Dennis explains about God and faith to her. Here Dennis
presents the heart of Roe's sermonic theme:

> "Faith is beyond reason, beyond knowledge, though not contrary
> to them. You are judging as we do not judge about the commonest
> affairs,—from a few, isolated, mysterious facts, instead of looking the
> subject all over. You pass by what is plain and well understood to

what is obscure, and from that point seek to understand Christianity. Every science has its obscure points and mysteries, but who begins with those to learn the science? Can you ignore the fact that millions of highly intelligent people, with every motive to learn the truth, have satisfied themselves as to the reality of our faith? Our Bible system of truth may contain much that is obscure, even as the starry vault has distances that no eye or telescope can penetrate, and as this little earth has mysteries that science cannot solve, but there is enough known and understood to satisfy us perfectly. Let me assure you . . . that Christianity rests on broad truths, and is sustained by arguments that no candid mind can resist after patiently considering them." (416)

Christine listens intently to Dennis and understands what he is saying about faith, but she still does not believe. She cries out, "If I could believe as you do, I should be the happiest of the happy." Dennis believes that in time this faith will come about, and he says, "I believe that the God of whom we have spoken *can directly reveal Himself to you* and make His truth as real to you as it is to me" (423). As Roe comments, "In the light of the terrible conflagration many things stood out with a distinctness that impressed her as nothing had ever done before. Wealth and rank had shrivelled to their true proportions . . ." (419). Christine sees this as she says aloud to herself, "That which can vanish in a night in flame and smoke cannot belong to us, is not a part of us. All that has come out of the crucible of this fire is my character, myself" (419). The "crucible of affliction" for Christine has been both the outer turmoil of the Chicago holocaust and her inner spiritual conflict—the struggle within her between the pagan teachings of her father and the unselfish love and Christian faith of Dennis. Searching for an answer, Christine asks Dennis for further guidance. He suggests that they pray together, and she agrees.

Later, after night falls, Dennis follows his mother's advice and prays for Christine. He stops when both he and Christine hear a woman groaning in pain. Dennis discovers that she is German and cannot speak or understand much English. Returning to Christine, he says, "The poor woman you have heard is sick and alone. She is German, and you can speak to her and comfort her as only a woman can." Dennis hopes that "in seeking to help another, might not Christine find help herself, and in the performance of a good deed, might not the Author of all good reveal Himself?" Christine is caught by surprise when the woman pleads, "Would you please say a little prayer for a lone sick body?" Amazed, Dennis watches Christine "kneel at the woman's side, lift her white face to heaven, and her lips move. Her attitude was unmistakably that of prayer. He could scarcely believe his eyes." From the teachings of his mother and from his own spiritual experiences, Dennis knows that prayer is mighty, but even he is astonished by Christine's actions. "Suddenly she clasped her hands and looked up with an ecstatic, thrilling cry: 'There is! there is! God lives and loves me, I feel, I know, and therefore I may hope and live.' Turning to the still raging flames, she exclaimed: 'Burn on with your fiery billows, I do not fear you now! I am safe, safe forever! Oh, how can I ever love and praise Thee enough!' Then, springing to Dennis's side, she took both his hands in hers." As they stand in the full radiance of both the Chicago fire and Christine's revelation, Christine thanks Dennis for helping her to find that God loves even her. "The look of love and gratitude she gave him will only find its counterpart in heaven, when the saved beam upon those who led them to the Saviour. The whole of her strong womanly soul, thoroughly aroused, was in her face, and it shone like that of an angel." Christine then turned back to the sick woman, "I think I can take better care of you now" (425–28).

The spiritual climax of *Barriers* has now been reached, for the religious conflict between Dennis and Christine has ended because God has answered their prayers. In the denouement Dennis gently tells Christine about the destruction of the Art Building and the sudden death of her father. Other explanations and discoveries follow. They uncover the duplicity of Christine's maid during Mrs. Fleet's illness and death. Christine also becomes aware of her father's machinations to mold her into a female August Ludolph. Then Christine in her actions and words expresses to Dennis her love for and gratitude to him, and her faith in God: "It seems that I have lost so little in this fire in comparison with what I have gained. And but for you I might have lost everything. How rich this first day of life, real, true life has been! My Heavenly Father has been so kind to me that I cannot express it. And to think how I have wronged Him all these years!" (439) She also states, "All that nonsense about the Baroness Ludolph is past forever,—burned up in the fire with many things of more value" (453). Dennis later finds Ernest Bruder and the other Bruder children and takes them under his care. Susie Winthrop, the mutual friend of Dennis and Christine, appears too, with the professor she had married shortly before the fire began. Bill Cronk, Dennis's good Samaritan, joins the group for a makeshift supper which Christine has prepared. Almost all the principal characters thus are together at the end of the novel, and, during the meal, Cronk, holding a large can full of coffee, offers a toast to Christine and Dennis, their future life, and to *"The United States of Ameriky!"* (464).

In the last chapter of the novel, "Every Barrier Burned Away," Dennis and Christine go to the ruins of the Art Building, the place where her father first cursed God and then burned to death. They there profess love for each other and make plans for the future. Although they are penniless they have hope for their life and faith in God's guidance. Roe concludes *Barriers* with emphasis on his theme: "What though the home before them is a deserted ruin? Love is joining hands that shall build a fairer and better one, because filled with that which only makes a home,—love. What though all around are only dreary ruins, where the night wind is sighing mournfully? Love has transformed that desert place into the paradise of God; and, if such is its power in the wastes of earthly desolation, what will be its might amid the perfect scenes of heaven?" (471). As Dennis and Christine face their future life, trusting in God's love, every barrier between the two young people has been burned away.

Barriers Burned Away: An Assessment

E. P. Roe's novels are generally well organized, with their main plots and subplots, conflicts, climaxes, denouements, foreshadowing, and suspense, all developed consistently and organically. Roe almost always uses an omniscient point of view, seeing all and knowing all. In *Barriers* he colors the novel with his own character and interests, his ethical values and moral beliefs, all influenced by his practical, everyday religious convictions. A serious criticism is that his characters are almost completely so-called stock characters: in Roe's favor, though, one must say that these characters are developed through action and dialogue, not by exposition. Christine's character growth throughout *Barriers* is an excellent illustration of Roe's capacity to present organic character development; her external fortune is completely changed, and so are her personal values and her beliefs about God.

Within Roe's novels are various kinds of conflict: man versus man or man versus woman (as Dennis versus Christine in *Barriers*); man versus society or the elements (as in *Barriers* Dennis fights to keep Christine and himself alive by not burning to death or drowning in the billowing water of the lake); and consistently, in all of Roe's novels, man versus God (in *Barriers,* August and Christine Ludolph when they first appear strongly believe that all religion is superstition and that God is a voodoo doctor).

Throughout *Barriers* Roe introduces subplots to add suspense and interest to his main story—the love Dennis has for Christine and his faith in God: Dennis struggling to rise in the world and trying to change the disdain Christine has for him, as well as hoping that Christine will someday recognize the need for God's guidance in her life. Roe's use of deus ex machina—the Chicago fire—brings Christine and Dennis together so each can at last recognize the true character of the other. Roe uses effective foreshadowing in his novels to prepare for the conclusions. The "crucible of affliction" in *Barriers* illustrates this skill. Taken together, the chapters are coherent and cohesive, and generally logical in their sequence of plot action, character development, and the final outcomes of the main plot and subplots. But chance is also common in *Barriers.* Bill Cronk appears suddenly to help Dennis rescue the young woman from the burning mansion, and he appears again at the end of the novel to give a toast, with coffee, at the makeshift meal.

Roe's descriptions of the Chicago fire are superior, for description appears to have been his forte here as it was in his *Evangelist* columns during the Civil War. All other descriptions are acceptable, though at times his tendency to exaggerate in order to make a point about the environment, natural or manmade, has amateurish results. Too often, also, when he needs description in order to add realism to his scenes, he omits some of the necessary background.

Roe's principal thematic impetus in *Barriers Burned Away*, as in all his novels, is to preach an interesting sermon that will hold the attention of his readers, and convincingly present the lifelong value of accepting the principles of Christ, and of having faith in God and His concern for those who follow His concepts. Although Roe became a full-time author, he never left the church pulpit. His love for God dominated him all his life, and his faith in divine guidance influenced his actions in all that he did, and especially as a minister-author.

Chapter Three

The Problem of Choice: Write or Preach

What Can She Do?

What had happened to Roe with his first novel, *Barriers Burned Away,* was extraordinary, and his overwhelming commercial success made him into a people's writer. Roe's readers liked his first novel and they were eager for the next one. In *Barriers* Roe had taken the religious novel, often a monotonous and wearisome narrative, and converted it from a task to a pleasure. Roe thus was forced by his reading public (and his own creative impulse) to begin another book. *What Can She Do?* was published in 1873, again with Dodd & Mead as publisher.

As before, Roe demonstrated his active social imagination, expressing in this second novel a strong concern for the equal role of women in the increasingly industrialized society of his day. In *What Can She Do?* he became a pioneer by calling attention to the need for equality of opportunity for the sexes. He also was applying his usual Christian principles. For Roe, practical religious beliefs of equality were essential in all strata of life. In his dedication to *What Can She Do?* Roe notes: "If I were to dedicate this book it would be to those girls who resolve that they will not play the poor role of Micawber, their only chance for life being that some one will 'turn up' whom they may burden with their helpless weight." He is explicit in the preface, condemning the education and treatment of women in his day:

This book was not written to amuse, to create purposeless excitement, or to secure a little praise as a bit of artistic work. It would probably fail in all these things. It was written with a definite earnest purpose, which I trust will be apparent to the reader. As society in our land grows older, and departs from primitive simplicity, as many are becoming rich, but more poor, the changes that I have sought to warn against become more threatening. The ordinary avenues of industry are growing thronged, and it daily involves a more fearful risk for a woman to be thrown out upon the world with unskilled hands, an untrained mind, and an unbraced moral nature. Impressed with this danger by some considerable observation, by a multitude of facts that might wring tears from stony eyes, I have tried to write earnestly if not wisely.

He warns against those men who would take a young girl's virtue and lead her into a life of promiscuity and sin.[1] This he calls "the 'skeleton in the closet' of society. But the evil exists on every side, and at some time or other threatens every home and life." He concludes his prefatory comments on a note of hope:

If I in my little sphere can by this book lead one father to train his children to be more strong and self-reliant, one mother to teach her daughters a purer, more patient, more heroic womanhood—if I have placed one more barrier in the tempter's way, and inspired one more wholesome fear and principle in the heart of the tempted— . . . if I can add one iota toward a public opinion that will honor useful labor, however humble, and render disgraceful idleness and helplessness, however gilded—if, chief of all, I lead one heavy-laden heart to the only source of rest, I shall be well rewarded, whatever is said of this volume.[2]

The plot of *What Can She Do?* involves three young sisters— Edith, Zell, and Laura Allen, daughters of a rich New York businessman. Their mother is a spoiled, selfish society woman who spends her husband's money recklessly. The three daughters have little more to interest them than social affairs and travel, and they have no training or education of any worth. Mr. Allen through a careless deal faces blackmail or exposure for defrauding the government of at least a million dollars. His worries over these charges culminate at a large party at his home, where he has a heart attack and dies when he learns that his colleagues and associates now know of the fraud.

The result of his death is devastating to his wife and daughters. Forced to move out of their expensive home, they cut back drastically on their wasteful expenditures. Soon they find themselves with hardly any money, and none is trained to earn a living or capable of doing any kind of work. "They were unable to cope with the practical questions of their situation. They had been launched upon the perilous[,] uncertain voyage of life, without the compass of a true faith, or the charts of principle to guide them, and in case of disaster, they had been provided with no life-boats of knowledge to save them" (115). The seventeen-year-old daughter, Zell, runs away with a dissolute sophisticate named Guillian Van Dam, who has promised to marry her (though he never does). The second daughter, Laura, a little older than Zell, is apathetic, vain, and selfish, interested more in her romances than in helping the family in any way. She is almost completely dependent upon Edith, the oldest daughter, who is described as "hard and pitiless" in her strength of purpose.

The mother and the three young women have to give up their Fifth Avenue home and move to the small place in the country that Edith's father had given her as a family joke after picking it up in a business arrangement. Here Edith tries amateurishly to start a small home-garden business. She believes she can make enough to support the household if she learns how to grow fruits and vegetables. Thanks to the help and kindness of an older man, a local gardener named Malcolm McTrump, she learns how to cultivate and tend her garden.

McTrump speaks with a Scottish accent; once more Roe, as one of his standard novelistic practices, has added a character who speaks unusual English. Another character added for humor and dialect is the Allens' old black butler, Hannibal, who is faithful to the family and stays with the women even after they move to the country. Hannibal practices Roe's helpful, everyday kind of religion: " 'De good Lord keep you safe, Miss Edie,' said Hannibal, tremblingly. 'You'se know I'd die for you in a minit; but I'se couldn't watch for a spook nohow . . .' " (346).

Arden Lacey, a young man in the country neighborhood, helps Edith with her gardening and falls in love with her. Like Dennis Fleet in *Barriers Burned Away,* Arden has strong character principles. Although he has been reared in a farm family where the father is a drunkard, he has developed, thanks to his mother, much interest in reading and learning, and he has staunch practical standards to guide his life. He had hoped to attend college (he has studied Latin, Greek, and other subjects, and is prepared for higher education), but he remains at home to protect his mother from her drunken and abusive husband and to work on the family farm. Arden is the so-called "spook" referred to by Hannibal for, unknown to Edith, he comes to her garden by moonlight and maintains it as often as he can without being discovered by anyone. Edith is determined to make a success of her small business: "Honest work is before me. . . . I will compel the world to give me a place at least, entitled, to respect" (347). Thanks to McTrump, she believes she can succeed in her efforts. From old McTrump she also receives understanding and practical advice about God. She asks him why God lets so many people suffer: " 'Bless your heart, puir child, He suffered mair than ony on us,' said Malcolm tenderly. 'But ye'll learn it a' soon. He who fled the famishin would bid ye eat noo' " (342).

Edith at last discovers that Arden has been the unknown good Samaritan who has cared for her garden while she has been asleep. Coming upon him in her garden, after sitting up awake most of one night, Edith imperiously demands, " 'By what right are you doing this work?' Then . . . [Arden's] own proud, passionate spirit flamed up, and looking her unblenchingly in the face, he replied: 'The right of my great love for you. Can I not serve my idol?' An expression of deep pain and revulsion came out upon Edith's face, and he saw it." Edith Allen has thought of Arden as a country peasant far beneath her Fifth Avenue upbringing (similar to the Christine Ludolph-Dennis Fleet relationship in *Barriers Burned Away*). Arden's love for Edith is a shock to her: "The avowal of his love was so abrupt—indeed it was almost stern and, coming thus from quite a stranger, who had so little place even in her thoughts, it was exceedingly painful, that it was like a blow. . . . And yet she hardly knew how to answer him, for she saw in his open, manly face, his respectful manner, that he meant no evil, however he might err through ignorance or feeling." When Edith replies, she has seen Arden's good intentions. " 'You have done wrong. . . . Remember I have no father or brother to protect me. The world is too ready to take up evil reports, and your strange action might be misunderstood. All transactions with me must be like the sunlight.' With an expression of almost anguish,

Arden bowed his head before her, and groaned, 'Forgive me; I did not think.' 'I am sure you meant no harm,' said Edith, with real kindness now in her tone" (366–68).

Several days later Edith receives a letter of apology and explanation from Arden. She goes to her neglected Bible for counsel, for, thanks to McTrump, she is now turning to God for comfort and strength. In her reply to Arden, Edith thanks him for his kindnesses and in return offers him "friendship" and "friendliness" (379). Overworked, Edith becomes ill, and during her convalescence she meditates on her life and her understanding of God. The McTrumps have told her to be consoled by the "Gude Book," as Edith tells Laura: "I continued to read eagerly about Him, till at last I felt I could venture to go to Him. So, I just bowed my head, on His invitation. . . . And how wonderfully He did help me." Edith believes that God now will help her family and her, for "I can leave all to Him. He is God; He loves, and He can, and will, take care of us" (389–90). Edith tells McTrump about her revelation. "God be praised!" he said. "I gie ye the right hond o' fellowship an welcome ye into the kirk o' the Lord. Ye noo belong to the household o' faith, an God's true Israel, an may His gude Spirit guide ye into all truth" (404). She is overwhelmed by his words, which to her become a benediction: "A sudden feeling of solemnity and awe came over Edith, and she felt as if she were crossing the mystic threshold and entering the one true church consisting of all believers in Christ" (404).

After recovering from her illness, Edith decides to find Zell, who has been violated and abandoned by Van Dam. During her search Edith encounters Mrs. Hart, a rich woman who devotes her time and wealth to help others. While helping Zell, who has had smallpox and is in a charity hospital ward, Edith is invited to stay at the Harts' home. There she meets Mr. Hart, a prosperous businessman who has carefully planned the education and practical preparation for life of his five daughters. One daughter is an accomplished musician and is qualified to teach music; another is studying drawing and painting and could teach drawing if needed; all five have been prepared to support themselves. They have had at-home lessons from skilled teachers in dressmaking, hairdressing, cooking, marketing, housekeeping. Here Roe draws a sharp contrast between the careless man-

ner in which the Allens reared and educated their daughters
and the concerned direction the Harts have given their daughters.

After Edith brings Zell to her home in the country, the
weather turns excessively dry and Edith believes that God has
forgotten her and wants to punish her for her early life. She
sees her garden withering under the hot sun, and she daily
looks for the needed rain. She needs money to pay the mortgage
on the small house, which she signed in desperation when her
money was almost depleted. Arden Lacey comes forth once
more to help Edith temporarily, bringing "a great barrel on
wheels, which was drawn by a horse" to water her garden,
and especially her biggest cash crop, her strawberries. As Edith
tells him he is as kind as a brother to her, "Her eyes grew
lustrous with admiration, gratitude, hope, and—yes, *love,* for
before the June twilight deepened into night it was revealed
in the depths of her heart that she loved Arden Lacey . . ."
(488). Soon rain comes to the countryside, saving Edith's vegetables and strawberries. The strawberries grow rapidly, and Edith
sells them at a profit, enabling her to pay off some of the mortgage and to take care of all the Allens. In the last chapter Arden
marries Edith, and they farm the land so that their gardens
and orchards pay off the mortgages on both the Arden and
Lacey homesteads.

Roe develops the plot and characters in *What Can She Do?*
in a melodramatic and predictable manner. But, although this
novel is not nearly so well constructed as *Barriers Burned Away,*
it still has a commendable, and even by today's standards, a
modern theme in Roe's view of practical training for young
girls to enable them to make a living in the world. When Zell
finds herself discarded in the city by Van Dam, she is unable
to find work of any kind except as a waitress. Rose Lacey, Arden's
younger sister, near the end of the story tries to make her own
way in the city, but she too finds the odds against her even
after she locates a shop-girl's job in a large store. As a clerk
on her feet all day and having to dress acceptably in order to
keep her job, Rose finds that six dollars a week is not enough
to live on. When she is ill for a week, Rose is evicted from
her boardinghouse. Defeated by her inadequate training, Rose
returns home. Edith, the once-rich city girl, also experiences

problems as she tries to earn money after she moves to the country. Roe in these instances emphasizes the need for young women to be practically prepared for life, and he contrasts the inadequate education of the Allen sisters and Rose Lacey with the training and preparation of the young women in the Hart family.

Roe included in *What Can She Do?* interconnected short sermons on the love of God, with everyone needing to trust the Supreme Being. Within the sermonic theme of *What Can She Do?* he speaks out for equality of all people, no matter their color, as when Edith, after finding her faith in God, talks frequently with Hannibal, the Allens' black servant. Typical of his novels, in *What Can She Do?* Roe uses an act of God to resolve a crisis in the plot—the coming of the much-needed rain for Edith's strawberries, her hope for success in her first business venture. The reading public bought *What Can She Do?* by the thousands, and once more Roe was a success. Much to his continuing surprise as well as to that of his publishers, this novel and all his others had large and regular sales throughout his lifetime.

Opening a Chestnut Burr

In 1874 Roe's third novel, *Opening a Chestnut Burr,* was published. Its main story involves Walter Gregory and his debilitating and psychologically unsettling mental depression. As the novel begins, Gregory is critically disappointed and upset, to the point of serious illness, with his career and his fortune. He has reached a nadir in living and is close to being suicidal.

In the preface to *Opening a Chestnut Burr* Roe remarks: "Must there not be something fatally wrong in that scheme of life which finds an heir of eternity weary, listless, discouraged, while yet in the dawning of existence? It is not in perishing *things,* merely, to give back the lost zest. But a glad zest and hopefulness might be inspired even in the most jaded and *ennui*-cursed, were there in our homes such simple, truthful natures as that of my heroine; and in the sphere of quiet homes—not elsewhere—I believe that woman can best rule and save the world."3

Gregory temporarily leaves his business position and goes to the country to regain his health, strength, and interest in life. He gets well while staying at his former country home, where he has been generously made welcome by the John Walton family and their saintlike daughter, Annie, who is Gregory's age. By the end of the novel Walter and Annie have overcome several difficulties, including Gregory's complete lack of faith in God. At the outset Gregory had looked down upon the kind Waltons with their unsophisticated pleasures, their love of nature, and their trust in God as shown daily through their evening family prayers. The main complication in the story involves Charles Hunting, a former friend who has cheated Gregory in a business transaction and is the cause of his bitterness. Unknown to Gregory, Hunting is engaged to Annie Walton, who believes Hunting is an honorable man. She does not know of his crooked dealings.

One night a crisis occurs at the Waltons. Flying cinders set the Walton home on fire. With complete concern for the Waltons and little for his own life, and with the help of Jeff, a black man on the Walton place, Gregory climbs on the roof and saves the house from burning, but he is hurt in doing so. While recovering from his injuries, he and Annie Walton talk about religion, and Gregory begins to heal in both body and spirit. During his convalescence Gregory discovers to his surprise that he is in love with Annie. Annie, true to her promise to Hunting to be his wife, tries to deny her growing affection for Gregory. Through their discussions of faith Gregory and Annie grow close to each other. One of their strongest bonds is their love for natural beauty, as well as their attachment to the home and area where Gregory was born and where Annie and her father now live. After his complete recovery, Gregory returns to the city healthy in body, mind, and spirit, and because of Annie's efforts, he is now trying to accept Christianity. He reads the Bible she has given him, and he does mission work. The disturbing areas of his life now are his unreciprocated love for Annie and the constant remembrance of Hunting's violation of what appeared to be true friendship.

As in many of Roe's other novels, a deus ex machina resolves plot and character entanglement. Through a series of events well prepared by Roe, Gregory, Annie, and Hunting are on the same Europe-bound ocean liner when it encounters a severe storm. While Gregory is on the deck on a stormy night, he

sees another ship come through the misty waves and strike the
steamship. During the rush for lifeboats Gregory stops to save
Hunting who is trapped in his stateroom. Gregory also helps
wherever he can, while Hunting cowers in fear, thinking of
his own safety. In the final scenes of the shipwreck all three
characters are almost drowned but manage to survive. Hunting
is later exposed as a cheat by a mutual business associate of
his and Gregory's. Soon after, Annie becomes betrothed to
Gregory, who finds his true self by becoming a Christian.

Roe ends the novel as he began it in the preface, with several
lines of poetry. Gregory and Annie now are married and planning to live in Gregory's home at Highlands on the Hudson.
Returning there one day from the city, Gregory gives his wife
this framed stanza:

> God sent His messenger of faith,
> And whispered in the maiden's heart,
> "Rise up and look from where thou art,
> And scatter with unselfish hands
> Thy freshness on the barren sands
> And solitudes of death."
>   O beauty of holiness,
>   Of self-forgetfulness!

As Gregory puts his arms around Annie, he says, "You are
the maiden, and God sent you to me" (545–46).

Once more Roe had written a commercial and popular success.
The reading public bought thousands of copies of his newest
book, and his career as a writer was firmly established. He now
found himself at a crossroads in his life, for in 1874 he realized
he had to decide between being a minister or being a novelist.

Resignation from the Ministry

While writing *Opening a Chestnut Burr,* Roe became ill from
overwork, and his personal physician urged the now-famous
patient to give up either writing or preaching. Reluctantly, Roe
gave up his new church in Highland Falls. He felt both happiness
and sorrow at leaving his parish of nine years. "As soon as
spring comes in reality, and the embargo of ice and snow is

over, we must be upon the wing; and this spontaneous proof of the friendliness of my people was very grateful to me." He remembered his congregation's generosity: "They have often been asked to give beyond their means" in order to build the new church and parsonage. "When I remember how patiently they have borne these burdens, how hard many have worked, and how many instances of self-denial there have been, I feel that too much cannot be said in their praise."[4]

It is clear that much could be said in praise of E. P. Roe, minister. His generous efforts are suggested in a letter written to Mary Roe after her brother's death by a devoted friend, Dr. Edgar A. Mearns, U.S. Army. Mearns and Roe had been planning another outdoor vacation together:

We were to walk through the woodlands, drive over the mountains, and sail on our native Hudson. I saw in mental vision the very rock under which we used to poke at the woodchucks with a stick, and on which we gathered the walking fern, and seemed once more to hear him discoursing of small fruits in his delightful garden, or reading to the family circle from his latest manuscripts. In the West many hearts have been pierced by this sorrow, for he made friends wherever he went.

Mearns believed that he knew "the private life" of his friend: "I have known him as a pastor, laboring assiduously among the members of his flock, dispensing liberal charity among the poor, and lightening everybody's burden. He was a rock to lay hold of when other friendships were borne away. . . ." Mearns remarked about Roe's dedication in giving all he could, including his life if needed, for his fellowman.

I have seen him as a hero, struggling in the water and broken ice, bearing in his arms the bodies of children for whom he risked his life. He had heard a cry for help, and that alone was enough to enlist the sympathy and secure the highest sacrifice of which our nature is capable. Then, paying no heed to personal sickness and injury, he strove to comfort the bereaved hearts of mothers, whose boys were drowned, perhaps by exposure laying the seeds of the disease which recently caused his death.[5]

What Roe did in real life—unselfishly risking his life for others—he had his fictional characters do in his novels. Dennis

Fleet in *Barriers Burned Away* during the Chicago fire saves
many lives and almost loses his own. Walter Gregory in *Opening
A Chestnut Burr* jeopardizes his health and life to extinguish a
roof fire on the Waltons' home; he also saves the lives of Annie
Walton and Charles Hunting during the collision at sea. More
significantly, Roe's heroes perform feats of bravery not for the
plaudits of the world but for the benefit of their fellowman.

After leaving his church, Roe bought an old-fashioned country
home with considerable acreage at Cornwall-on-the-Hudson,
two miles from his childhood home, where he continued to
write and where he cultivated small fruits. At the beginning
of his writing years Roe had used his home gardening as extra
income in the support of his family. Mary Roe remembered
her brother's success with strawberries: "When the vines were
bearing, sometimes as many as forty bushels of berries were
picked in a single day. Some of them were of mammoth size.
I remember, on one occasion, we took from a basket four berries
which filled to the brim a large coffee-cup, and notwithstanding
their enormous size they were solid and sweet."[6] Roe also wrote
for *Scribner's Magazine* on his strawberry gardens, and Dodd
& Mead collected and published these articles in 1880 as *Success
with Small Fruits.*

While at Cornwall, Roe transplanted flowers and shrubs (and
some of his mother's rose bushes) from his boyhood home to
his new home, with his eighty-year-old father helping and de-
lighting in the growth of the plants. Yet what grew best out
of Roe's home in Cornwall were many novels, almost one a
year until 1888. But still he was perplexed as to whether he
should have left his church. Letters and newspaper articles "severely criticised him," reported Mary Roe, "for giving up the
ministry." Roe said to her, after reading all of the numerous
letters he regularly received from men and women who had
read his novels, "These are mostly from young men, not one
of whom I know, who have written to me of the benefit received
from my books." At that moment, as Mary Roe recalled, her
brother established firmly in his heart that he would stand fast
to his decision to leave his church and become a full-time novelist. Yet he never completely left his minister's position, for "he
was always ready to preach when needed, especially in neglected
districts," and, after his father died, he taught his father's Sunday
school class.[7]

Although he was concerned about leaving his pulpit, the letters he received from those who had read his novels and who had been inspired to lead a better life because of them convinced him that he had made the right decision. His final statement on this matter is positive:

I know my books are read by thousands; my voice reached at most a few hundred. I believe many who would never think of writing to me such letters as these are also helped. Do you think I have made a mistake? My object in writing, as in preaching is to do good, and the question is, Which can I do best? I think with the pen, and I shall go on writing, no matter what the critics say.[8]

Chapter Four

The People's Writer

After Roe left his parish at Highland Falls and settled into his new home at Cornwall-on-the-Hudson, he wrote prodigiously until his sudden death in 1888. His daily schedule indicates how much time, energy, and preparation he put into his books: "My methods of work are briefly these. I go into my study immediately after breakfast, usually about nine o'clock, and write or study until three or four in the afternoon, stopping only for a light lunch. In the early morning and late afternoon I go around my place, giving directions to the men, and observing the condition of vegetables, flowers, and trees, and the general aspect of nature at the time. After dinner, the evening is devoted to the family, friends, newspapers, and light reading." When Roe was younger, he often wrote many more hours each day. "In former years I wrote at night, but after a severe attack of insomnia this practice was almost wholly abandoned. As a rule, the greater part of a year is absorbed in the production of a novel, and I am often gathering material for several years in advance of writing."

Roe was also a careful workman, for "after correcting the manuscript," as he wrote, "it is put in type-writing and again revised. There are also two revisions of the proof" (*NA*, 493). There are anecdotes about Roe's meticulous attention to his novels' proofs, all the way to the printing presses. E. D. Walker commented on this practice: "He carried his corrections even into the composing department of his publisher, often taking the proof-reader's place and making changes just before the type was sent to the pressroom." Walker presented too an observation on Roe's writing procedure: "It was his custom to write out the chapters of his novels on slips and then have them copied on typewriters. The original slips look very much like the slips on which Dickens wrote his copy. They are almost illegible owing to the great number of erasions, corrections, etc. Mr. Roe was a believer in Ben Jonson's saying: 'Easy writing makes hard reading.' "[1]

Roe not only wrote steadily each year but he also daily supervised an expanding vegetable and fruit business that he looked after personally. At first he would not depend on his literary earnings to take care of his family, and he therefore used his land for extensive cultivation. There on twenty-three acres he grew many fruits and vegetables, including pears, apples, grapes, and strawberries. He had seventy varieties of strawberries and over one hundred of grapes.

In 1882 Roe gave up active participation in his garden/farm projects in order to deal with heavy financial losses within his family. As Mary Roe records, "Owing to the failure of an elder brother [in the hotel business in Cornwall] . . . , Edward, in his efforts to help him, became deeply involved, and to satisfy his creditors was obliged to sell the copyrights of several of his earlier books."[2] To Roe, this was first a time for sorrow because of his insolvency, but very soon afterwards a time for rejoicing. "There came a date when all my interests in my books then published must be sold to the highest bidder. It seemed in a sense like putting my children up at auction; and yet I was powerless, since my interests under contracts were a part of my assets. These rights had been well advertised in the New York and county papers, as the statute required, and the popularity of the books was well known." Much to the surprise of both Edward and Mary Roe, a friend bought all the rights by making the highest bid, and, once more, one of the staunch friendships that Roe had made all through his life came forth to help him. "My rights in the first nine novels became his, legally and absolutely. There was even no verbal agreement between us,—nothing but his kind, honest eyes to reassure me. He not only paid the sum he had bidden, but then and there wrote a check for a sum, which, with my other assets, immediately liquidated my personal debts, principal and interest." After several years Roe could write, "The children of my fancy are again my children, for they speedily earned enough to repay my friend and to enable him to compromise with the holders of endorsed notes in a way satisfactory to them" (*NA*, 495–96).

By 1886 over one million copies of Roe's books had been purchased in the United States, "to which nearly one-half of that number may be added as representing their sale in England, Canada, Australia and the different languages into which they have been translated."[3] Frequently there were adverse reviews, which Roe recognized and accepted, but many favorable reviews praised his novels for their moral purpose, imaginative plot, admirable characterization, dramatic power, absorbing descriptions, stirring scenes—in general, for being a refreshing change from the average dull and boresome religious novel. Roe had become a well-established and successful author.

He was so successful, in fact, that he received the ultimate accolade of acceptance—imitation. Uncharacteristically, Roe satirically wrote about his "double"—about the "one who appears willing to stick closer to me than a brother." Both the name of Roe and the covers of his books were imitated: "A certain 'Edward R. Roe' is also an author, and is suffering cruelly in reputation because his publishers so manage that he is identified with me. By strange coincidence, they hit upon a cover for his book which is almost a fac-simile of the cover of my pamphlet novel 'An Original Belle,' previously issued. The R in the name of this unfortunate man has been furnished with such a diminutive tail that it passes for a P, and even my friends supposed that the book, offered everywhere for sale, was mine." When Roe asked questions of booksellers, he received replies that he expected. "In many instances I have asked at news-stands, 'Whose book is that?' The prompt and invariable answer has been, 'E. P. Roe's.' I have seen book-notices in which the volume was ascribed to me in anything but flattering terms." With rare sarcasm Roe wrote, "My publishers, Messrs. Dodd, Mead & Co., with their lawyers, are coming to his [E. R. Roe's] aid in a suit to enjoin the publication in its present guise of the book which is perilling his reputation, if not mine. Let me suggest to the Western Roe that he find publishers who will permit him to shine undimmed by the shadows cast by my literary sins" (NA, 496). After Roe's death this suit against E. R. Roe came to court, as Walsh explained: "[Roe] would have been surprised, indeed, if he had lived, to learn that the Western court dismissed his petition for an injunction, and that a reported obiter dicta of the learned judge who decided the case was to the effect that he had never seen a more flimsy pretext for an injunction. If the Western States [as Matthew Arnold earlier wrote] are indeed nourished upon the writings of an author called Roe, they do not seem to have taken to heart the lesson of uprightness and justice which those writings aim to teach."[4]

Paul R. Cleveland, writing in *Cosmopolitan* in 1888, summarized Roe's career: "Financially he is a giant among lilliputians as to manuscript making. It sounds incredible; but I am authoritatively informed that the royalty from his works for the last year reached forty thousand dollars. Not since Cooper, probably, has any native author's works found such a host of friends."[5] By 1888 Roe had sent his sermons through his novels to millions of readers—sermons that encouraged them to lead a good life, to follow the example set by Christ, and to have faith in God's guidance.

"Gentle Woman Roused"

Before examining the remainder of Roe's novels, it is useful to consider an 1874 short story. The story shows Roe's continuing concern for the importance of woman's influence in everyday life, and the pressing need for women to step out of their generally accepted and expected roles as wives and mothers whose place is only in the home. Just as he did in *What Can She Do?*, Roe once more spoke out for women's rights. The title of the story identifies his theme: "Gentle Woman Roused—Story of the Temperance Movement in the West." Roe here endorsed the woman's temperance movement and its early use of public prayers to denounce the sale and use of intoxicating liquor. (Carry Moore Nation [1846–1911], it should be noted, did not begin her nationally famous involvement in the temperance movement until 1877, and she did not receive considerable national newspaper coverage for her advocacy of temperance until she and her followers began their zealous destruction of saloon property and liquor.)

In "Gentle Woman Roused" Nellie Elliott belatedly learns that her husband Vinton is an alcoholic and spends most of his evenings at Harry Hill's, and not, as Vinton says, at his law office. After a day of soul-searching Nellie organizes a group of women to walk as a body to Harry Hill's plush "drinking-

saloon," described by Roe as "elegant" in all its appointments
and "frequented by gentlemen." What Nellie then does contra-
dicts her statements at the beginning of the story: "The idea
of women marching in bands through the streets, followed by
a rabble of rude men and boys; the idea of refined ladies forcing
their way into some filthy bar-room, full of obscene, guzzling,
ill-omened looking loafers, and [then] kneeling on the tobacco-
stained floor in audible prayer!" But this is what she does as
she forcefully confronts Harry Hill and finally convinces him
to close his establishment. Vinton is upset by what he has done
to harm his marriage, and, because of Nellie's unusual actions,
he gives up drink. But the strain on Nellie has been harmful
to her health, and soon Vinton is grief-stricken over his wife's
lingering illness. Her fate is unknown: "What the end will be
God only knows."[6]

Within this simple short story Roe demonstrates once more
his conviction that religion should have a cutting edge to it.
During his entire lifetime he was known to be good and kind
but also just and firm. He stated that women should have a
responsible voice in the affairs of the world; he was convinced
that believers in Christ, such as Dennis Fleet in *Barriers Burned
Away* and Nellie Elliott in "Gentle Woman Roused," should
march forward as soldiers of God to help their fellowman. In
this short story as in the novels, Roe's religious message is direct
and consistent.

Eight More Novels

From 1875 to early 1884 Roe wrote and published eight
novels, some of them first published as periodical serials: *From
Jest to Earnest* (1875), *Near to Nature's Heart* (1876), *A Knight
of the Nineteenth Century* (1877), *A Face Illumined* (1877), *A
Day of Fate* (1880), *Without a Home* (1881), *His Sombre Rivals*
(1883), *A Young Girl's Wooing* (1884). In 1876 he also wrote
a pamphlet, *A Manual on the Culture of Small Fruits,* and in 1880
Dodd & Mead published *Success with Small Fruits.* Roe was prodigiously writing and publishing, and he was dominating the best-
selling lists. In 1881 *Barriers Burned Away,* in a printing by
Dodd & Mead of 100,000 copies at twenty cents apiece, was
still selling as though it were a newly published novel. Dodd
& Mead also issued under the editorship of Lyman Abbott *The*

Roe Birthday Book: Birthday Mottoes Selected from the Writings of E. P. Roe. Like Roe's other books, this one sold well.

From Jest to Earnest (1875). In *From Jest to Earnest* Roe returns to his home region and sets his story in "Highland on the Hudson." The novel tells of Lottie Marsden, a rich, carefree young woman who plays a practical joke (the "jest" of the story) on Frank Hemstead, a serious young ministerial student whose ambition is to be a "home missionary" in a small community in the West. Lottie is a child of luxury, the self-assured sophisticate who has few if any religious beliefs, and Frank is like a young Abraham Lincoln, tall, gangly, unworldly. Frank through relatives meets Lottie at a Christmas party, and she pretends to fall in love with him in order to make him out a fool because of his religious principles. She also wants to prove her womanly wiles to her laughing friends, whom she has informed of what she plans to do with Frank.

The novel is full of light repartee, and Roe supplies an abundance of puns, most of them referring to Frank's unusual Lincolnesque height and innocent vulnerability. Lottie delights in toying with Frank's sincere feelings as she fulfills her social role as a fashionable and wealthy young lady from New York. Her game continues through most of the novel until Frank learns of her heartless and deliberate jest. When he confronts her with this accusation, she is stunned, for she has failed to see how cruel she has been. This confrontation scene awakens Lottie and causes her to see her artificial and destructive life. In desperation she goes to her Bible, which Frank had earlier encouraged her to read. The climax of the novel occurs when Frank and Lottie and several other young people are snowbound one night when their sleigh overturns in a drift. Through this experience Lottie sees Frank's honest nature and responds to the hardships of the night with the best in her character. Lottie and Frank converse a great deal during this snowy and cold experience, and eventually Lottie finds her feelings for Frank being converted from jest to earnest.

From Jest to Earnest is one of Roe's lightweight novels, and his wit holds full sway. Most of the favorable criticism it received called attention to its bright vivaciousness and frolicking wit, as well as Frank Hemstead's strong resemblance to Abraham Lincoln.

Near to Nature's Heart (1876). *Near to Nature's Heart*
is a story of the American Revolution. The novel begins on
17 June 1776, in the granite mountains around the Hudson
Highlands. The hero is Theron Saville who, while on a lone
canoe trip up the Hudson, comes upon a beautiful young
woman, Vera Brown, who is an untouched child of nature.
How these two finally come together and marry takes up a
large portion of a complicated plot structure. Of principal interest is the appearance of General George Washington in the
revolutionary battles. Like the novelists of today, Roe shows
Washington in scenes where the general symbolizes the fighting
Americans and where he speaks out against the skeptics who
doubt the truth of the Bible.

Roe's descriptions of nature and of military battles are excellent, and his backgrounds in both—of nature from his family,
of the military from his Civil War service—are clearly evident.
The descriptions give authenticity to *Near to Nature's Heart.*

A Knight of the Nineteenth Century (1877). *A Knight of
the Nineteenth Century* is the story of Egbert Haldane and how
he progresses from a bad to a good knight. Haldane is a spoiled
young man of upper society who has been given much leeway
and luxury by his mother and not enough moral discipline and
Christian guidance. Haldane drinks excessively and is duped
several times when he is drunk. He meets attractive young Laura
Romeyn, whom he comes to love even though at first he makes
ill-mannered advances to her. When Haldane reaches an understanding with himself and begins to link his life with that of
Christ (he has been receiving religious guidance from older
friends), he decides to leave home but to stay in his hometown,
where he has a reputation as a wastrel and a "jailbird" (as he
is called at employment places). Helped by recluse Jeremiah
Growther, Haldane begins work as a laborer.

As he progresses economically he grows as a person, soon
becoming a medical student, then a doctor, and later serving
in the Union army during the Civil War, entering as a captain.
Because of his unusual capacities with the soldiers, acting as a
chaplain as well as a doctor, Haldane's good works become
known to the people back home, particularly those who had
read in the local newspaper about his escapades as a young
ne'er-do-well. Because of kindnesses he has shown to Laura's

relatives in a Southern community afflicted with a yellow-fever epidemic, she too learns that Haldane is a good knight who would give his life for others, just as Christ did while on earth. After they marry, Laura and Haldane stay in Hillaton, where Dr. Haldane is known as a "knightly man," serving all his patients but, like Christ, serving the poor and the hungry first. Included in this novel is Roe's advocacy of a simple religion, of living a good life. He also speaks out against sermons so clouded with excessive theology and philosophy that the minister and his words become separated from warmth and kindness. Several chapters in *A Knight of the Nineteenth Century* are larded with denunciations of churches that lack sincere hospitality for strangers—churches that are spiritually frigid because they lack sympathy for the poor and the other misfits of society. The open church Roe advocates in *A Knight of the Nineteenth Century* is similar to the kind of church Reverend Robert Collyer rebuilt physically and spiritually after the Chicago fire. Collyer, like Roe, preached the theme of personal religious life, and in his congregations all social classes could be found. (It was on the steps of Collyer's burned-out church that Roe meditated among Chicago's still-smoldering ruins.)

In *A Knight of the Nineteenth Century* Roe becomes an outspoken critic of religion as practiced by many of his fellow Christians. In this fifth novel he severely criticizes ministers, even choirs, that put on a routine and indifferent performance each Sunday in churches that fail to project the strength of God's guidance into the hearts of the congregation. This is Roe's message. It is almost the same kind of message William Faulkner presents in *Light in August* when Gail Hightower fails as a minister: the people in Hightower's church, as in many others, worship the physical aspects and appearances of religion, the church and not God Himself. Roe's criticism is similar: Make religion a personal involvement, not an impersonal and social obligation. Make God into what He can be to all Christians—a personal Friend and Guide to walk with through one's life.

A Face Illumined (1877). Roe wrote *A Face Illumined* several years after he had observed a lovely young woman at a concert. From a distance she made a striking appearance, but as Roe moved closer he saw that, although her face was beautiful, her facial expression was discordant and unattractive. This young

woman of Roe's real life becomes the fictional heroine, Ida
Mayhew, in *A Face Illumined,* and Roe in fiction becomes Harold
Van Berg, a rich and successful young artist who emphasizes
the spirit of goodness in the faces of his subjects. While listening
to a Beethoven selection at a concert, Van Berg becomes disturbed as he looks at Ida because, even though the physical
features of her face are beautiful, the expression is shallow.
Like Egbert Haldane in *A Knight of the Nineteenth Century,*
Ida Mayhew has been spoiled all her life, and simultaneously
neglected by her parents, who have given her what Roe calls
a sham for an education. Her mind therefore has not been
given an adequate opportunity to develop, and her potentially
good moral nature is unfulfilled. Throughout his story Roe refers
to her as a modern Undine. One remembers the folktale Undine,
the female water sprite who could acquire a soul only by marrying a good and faithful human being. Ida Mayhew is Undine,
and Harold Van Berg is the faithful follower of God and a
good man who eventually marries her.

Roe condemns the life Ida leads, for she is a superficial social
belle flirting with each desirable man she meets. When Van
Berg is indifferent to her wiles (he meets her, reluctantly,
through one of his cousins), Ida is perplexed, then intrigued.
When self-scrutiny enters her thinking, she questions the trivial
life she has been leading. After several troubling incidents with
Van Berg, situations that sometimes involve her characterless
beaus, Ida plans to change—her style of dress, her actions, her
attitudes. Humility and despair overcome her as she realizes
how cheap and insignificant her life has been. She attempts
suicide, once just stopping before swallowing a powerful opiate.
Because of her efforts to reform herself, Van Berg's opinion
of her wavers, and he becomes puzzled as to whether he has
judged her fairly.

The catalyst that causes Ida finally to see her true self is an
old man, James Eltinge, a lover of nature and believer in a
personal relationship with God; Ida's flip friends call Eltinge
"the Ancient Mariner." Eltinge presents Roe's sermons in *A
Face Illumined;* throughout several chapters Eltinge talks help-
fully to Ida. These religious lessons from Eltinge persuade Ida
that each person has to find an intimate relationship with God,
and that prayers are the means by which each can willingly

open his spirit to the Lord. This sermonic theme in *A Face Illumined* is similar to the message the Ancient Mariner in Coleridge's poem was committed to tell the world:

> He prayeth best, who loveth best,
> All things both great and small;
> For the dear God who loveth us,
> He made and loveth all.

Through the efforts of Eltinge, Ida realizes that her past life will not stop God from loving her, and she turns to Him for guidance. As she prays with her old friend one day, she jumps up and embraces him with love and thankfulness, exclaiming that she knows that God has heard her prayers, that now she can escape from the living death she formerly thought was life. Van Berg realizes that he has not been a good Christian in his pitiless attitude toward Ida; and, acknowledging that he had violated God's standards of compassion toward others, he apologizes to Ida for his unkindness. His generous action, added to the revelation to Ida by prayer of God's personal love for her, persuades her to think of living anew, and she discards the bottle of poison she had intended to use for her suicide.

Ida and Van Berg achieve full understanding after he is seriously injured while walking alone in dense, desolate woods. During his rescue and convalescence Van Berg and Ida discover their true love for each other and their mutual faith in God's love. The culminating scene takes place in Eltinge's garden, where the two young people (Van Berg on crutches) betroth their lives to each other.

The outstanding feature of *A Face Illumined* is the character of James Eltinge, a man of nature and a man of absolute kindness, goodness, and love. Roe's preface to this novel makes one realize that the character of the old man and the value of the garden are based on Roe's fond memories of his own father and his garden; it was Roe's father, one recalls, who instilled in Edward the boy affection for nature and God.

A Day of Fate (1880).   For his entire preface to *A Day of Fate* Roe quotes six words from Shakespeare, "Some shallow story of deep love." Departing from his usual omniscient point of view, he tells this story in the first person. The "I" in *A*

Day of Fate is Richard Morton, a New York newspaper editor who has brought himself close to a nervous breakdown by overwork and loss of interest in his life. Escaping from the city, Morton travels north in the state until he reaches a small town, where impetuously he attends a religious service at a Society of Friends meeting house. During the silent meeting he sees a young woman he feels is the perfect woman he has been searching for. When Morton is later made welcome by members of the church, he meets the Yocomb family and Morton's "perfect woman," their beautiful daughter, Adah. To his disappointment, he discovers after talking with Adah that she is a superficial young woman interested mainly in clothes and beaus.

The Yocombs are generous to Richard Morton and invite him to dinner. Their farmhouse fulfills all of his dreams, and it is evident to a reader of *A Day of Fate* that the farmhouse, the trees, the scenery around the home—all are modeled on Roe's boyhood memories. One of Yocomb's prized garden plots, it should be especially noted, is his strawberry bed. At dinner Morton meets Emily Warren, a rather plain-looking young woman who is a music teacher. She has been staying with the Yocombs for only a short time, and she is a woman of practical goodness and faith in God, as Morton learns. The Yocombs soon see that Morton needs rest and relaxation, and they treat him warmly.

The day of fate (the deus ex machina also) occurs that night when lightning and then fire strike the Yocomb home. Mr. and Mrs. Yocomb, Adah and her young sister Yillah, and Emily Warren are stunned and shocked by the lightning bolt. Morton and the teen-age Yocomb boy, Reuben, fight the fire, bring a doctor to the scene, and save the home and all lives. These happenings on Morton's "day of fate" cause him to fall in love with Emily Warren and rekindle his faith in God. He becomes ill after his night of extreme effort and speaks impetuously to Emily as she nurses him. When he tells her he loves her, she becomes upset, for reasons Morton later learns. She has agreed to marry an older man, Gilbert Hearn, a New York City banker who has helped her to find her way in life after the death of her parents. Because of her common sense, Emily later diplomatically writes to Hearn, telling him that she has mistaken her deep appreciation to him for abiding love. The story ends a year from the beginning, after Morton has returned, rejuvenated, to his city desk, and then comes back to the Yocombs and Emily for Thanksgiving dinner. Adah Yocomb and Gilbert Hearn have also found happiness, for they have discovered each other. Adah loves Hearn, and Hearn is greatly pleased to marry Adah, who loves him for himself and not for his wealth.

Besides the first-person point of view, *A Day of Fate* is noteworthy for Roe's controlled compression into a short time span— the day of fate—most of the motivating actions of the story. The organic growth of Morton's character is well handled, and Adah's progress from a silly country girl to a society matron is acceptable.

Again, Roe's religious theme is present in this novel. But in *A Day of Fate* his "sermons" are not too noticeable because he makes the Yocomb family and their membership in the Society of Friends the center of genuine goodness. The inner light, the Friends believe, comes only from God and then enters one's heart. Essentially this is Roe's own message: Pray to God to establish your awareness that God is personally concerned about you. Pray always, and as Mr. Fleet whispered on his deathbed in *Barriers Burned Away,* *"Whatever happens never lose faith in the goodness of God."* This is the message Richard Morton learns in *A Day of Fate,* the message of hope that Roe wrote for millions of his readers.

Without a Home (1881).   Ten years after Roe began his first novel, *Barriers Burned Away,* he brought out *Without a Home.* He took extra time to write this novel, which first appeared as a serial in the *Boston Congregationalist.* The main plot concerns two young people, Mildred Jocelyn and Roger Atwood; she is rich, he is poor. Their eventual declaration of love is complicated by Mildred's girlish infatuation for Vinton Arnold, a weakling who socially and financially is higher in society than she. Mildred is forced to make her own way in the world when her father's business fails, and she becomes a professional nurse, self-supporting and independent. During her two years' training as a nurse, Roger leaves his farm home and is graduated high in his class from a two-year college. Through circumstances Roe effectively foreshadows, Roger inherits a large sum of money from an uncle and becomes a wealthy man, then studies to become a lawyer.

When Vinton Arnold dies near the end of the novel, Roger is still trying to win Mildred's love. In the next-to-final chapter Roger, out taking a walk, risks his life to stop a runaway horse. In doing so, he critically injures himself and, before becoming unconscious, asks that he be taken to Bellevue Hospital where Mildred now is working. During his convalescence Mildred learns to love Roger, and at the end of the novel they are married.

The characters, plot, and overall development are generally well done, but Roe had other reasons for writing *Without a Home.* He wanted to call attention to the problems caused by opium addiction, to expose the deplorable working conditions of women in shops and stores, and to inform the public of the undesirable conditions in city tenements.

Because of Mildred's father's addiction to opium, he loses his business position and his money, forcing his family into poverty. Roe describes the pangs and final death of Jocelyn in extensive detail, hoping that his readers will take this message to heart. In order to be able to write about this destructive habit, Roe had read many books and consulted with medical doctors, as he wrote in the preface to *Without a Home:* "It will soon be discovered that the modern opium or morphia habit has a large place in this volume. While I have tried to avoid the style of a medical treatise, which could be in poor taste in a work of fiction, I have carefully consulted the best medical works and authorities on the subject, and I have conversed with many opium slaves in all stages of the habit." Roe's predictions about the problems of taking narcotic drugs have become disturbing realities in the twentieth century: "I am sure I am right in fearing that in the morphia hunger and consumption one of the greatest evils of the future is looming darkly above the horizon of society. Warnings against this poison of body and soul cannot be too solemn or too strong."[7]

Roe introduces his social criticism on the abuse of working women into *Without a Home* at the point where Mildred and her sister Belle are job-hunting. When they are hired as shopgirls, they work long hours for low pay and are forbidden to sit down all day. Besides being watched closely by their overseers, Belle and Mildred find that their coworkers treat them unconsiderately. They soon learn how the store's management heartlessly hires and fires the shop-girls with no concern for their working conditions or their rights as individuals.

In an unusual addition, Roe added an appendix to *Without a Home,* in which he directly spoke out against the unsatisfactory treatment of shop-girls. He appealed to store owners and retail merchants to supply places for women to rest and to eat their lunches, and to give them respite from the requirement that they stand by their store counters all day. Also, in both the novel and its appendix he addressed the crowded and undesirable conditions of tenements, stating that in such unsafe and unsanitary dwellings even the rudiments of life become difficult to sustain.

In *Without a Home* Roe, in some ways a nineteenth-century American Emile Zola, used fiction to criticize society for its failure to bring reforms. Despite its having a conventional romantic plot, *Without a Home* is a pioneering book because of its realistic consideration in fiction of tenement living, working rights for shop-girls, and the awful consequences of dope addiction. Modern critics, because of their ignorance of Roe's novels, have failed to acknowledge Roe as a well-informed critic of society.

***His Sombre Rivals* (1883).** The subtitle of *His Sombre Rivals* is *A Story of the Civil War.* What Roe wrote in the preface to this novel is worth quoting at length, for once more he demonstrated his capacity to view life objectively through a wide perspective.

The following story has been taking form in my mind for several years, and at last I have been able to write it out. . . . Although a Northern man, I think my Southern readers will feel that I have sought to do justice to their motives. At this distance from the late Civil War, it is time that passion and prejudice sank below the horizon, and among the surviving soldiers who were arrayed against each other I think they have practically disappeared. Stern and prolonged conflict taught mutual respect. The men of the Northern armies were convinced, beyond the shadow of a doubt, that they had fought men and Americans—men whose patriotism and devotion to a cause sacred to them was as pure and lofty as their own.

With characteristic love and faith, Roe continued in words that have Lincolnesque nuances:

It is time that sane men and women should be large-minded enough
to recognize that, whatever may have been the original motives of
political leaders, the people on both sides were sincere and honest;
that around the camp-fires[,] at their hearths and in their places of
worship they looked for God's blessing on their efforts with equal
freedom from hypocrisy.

In writing the battle scenes of *His Sombre Rivals* Roe used
historical records, his personal experiences, and his imagination:
"I have endeavored to portray the battle of Bull Run as it could
appear to a civilian spectator: to give a suggestive picture and
not a general description. The following war-scenes are imagi-
nary, and colored by personal reminiscence. I was in the service
nearly four years, two of which were spent in the cavalry."[8]

The public clamor for this new Roe book was so general
that publication was delayed by Dodd & Mead until 25,000
copies could be printed and placed on the market. While writing
his novel, Roe had often worked from breakfast until long after
midnight, and his long hours in writing again proved fruitful.
His Sombre Rivals sold rapidly, just as all his other novels did.

The book has one of Roe's best plots. Both Alford Graham
and Warren Hilland, close friends, are in love with the same
girl, Grace St. John. In order not to hurt his friend Graham
conceals his love for Grace. When Grace and Hilland marry,
Graham becomes Hilland's protector, even during the Civil
War. In battle Graham saves Hilland's life, almost losing his
own. But Hilland, a brave Union officer, is later killed, and
after the war, when Graham returns home a highly decorated
colonel, he finds Grace has become a victim of a form of amnesia
and has no will to live.

Graham consults with noted doctors, who decide Grace Hilland needs constant love and care from someone who loves
her or she will die. They advise Graham to marry Grace. Graham, after agonizing over his choice, marries her for the sake
of his dead friend and in order to save Grace's life. At the
end of the novel she regains her full mental capacity, and after
some time of adjustment, they truly become man and wife.
They move to Virginia, where he sets up a plantation near
Southerners who befriended him during the war. The Grahams
there become respected members of the community.

Again Roe displays his strength as a writer: the battle descriptions demonstrate his remarkable awareness of military men and their involvement in conflict. *His Sombre Rivals* is evidence that Roe the novelist was growing in skill and judgment. He still wrote much on the need to trust God, yet these sections are incorporated into the story with greater facility than ever before. Also, Roe's use of dialect characters in *His Sombre Rivals* is of good quality: he includes many blacks—soldiers, slaves, cooks, concerned and kind mammies—in the story.

A Young Girl's Wooing (1884). *A Young Girl's Wooing* has a simple plot. Madge Alden, left an orphan at age thirteen, is befriended by her older sister and her husband, Mary and Henry Muir. Madge meets Graydon Muir, Henry's college-age brother, when she comes to the Muir home to live. Grayson is kind and considerate, and he helps shy and unsure Madge feel welcome. But, despite the efforts of the three Muirs, Madge almost becomes a recluse and an invalid, with reading her main occupation, the books she reads superficial and of little value.

As Madge grows into young womanhood, she sees that her life is going nowhere and that her health is steadily failing. She realizes also that she is in love with Graydon, who considers her only as his sick little sister; he has extra time for her, but he treats her as though she is a little girl who will never grow up. When Graydon completes college, his brother Henry sends him to Europe on a business trip. Madge comes to Graydon's stateroom to say goodbye, and faints because of the unusual exertion. Graydon sails away, believing that Madge will die before he returns. The Henry Muirs then take strong action to restore her health, if possible. They consult doctors, who advise a change of climate and interests, and the Muirs send her to Santa Barbara, where they have long-time friends. In California Madge Alden grows strong and healthy through horseback riding, sports and other exercise, and she also becomes an attractive, mature, and level-headed woman with the capacity to use her mind. When she returns to the East, she discreetly "woos" Graydon Muir. Near the end of *A Young Girl's Wooing* the tables are turned on Graydon as he breaks his leg when hiking with Madge, and Madge, the former "weak little sister," handles his injury and his rescue with sensible preparation and foresight.

A Young Girl's Wooing is a surprise in Roe's creative development. Although it contains advice on the necessity for a good character in life, there is little that would make it a religious novel. Even though on the surface it appears to be only a light-hearted romance, it is much more: Roe continues to stress that women should be prepared for life and able to handle themselves during misfortunes and emergencies. Madge at the end of the novel represents Roe's belief that women should have practical knowledge in order to have a life equal with men. For example, she expresses no fear during a thunderstorm while other young women cringe in fear; in another situation she capably handles high-spirited horses while a group of women and men look on with trepidation. When Madge Alden returns from California, she steps forward in her life as one of Roe's ideally accomplished women—for she is independent, self-confident, and self-reliant, exactly what Roe had advocated earlier in *What Can She Do?*

The Last Novels—Late 1884–1888

When *A Young Girl's Wooing* was published in 1884, Roe's books were still selling in unusually high numbers. *A Young Girl's Wooing* was published in a hardcover first edition of 25,000 copies. The other novels were also being bought as though they had just been published. Two of the earliest novels, *Barriers Burned Away* (1872) and *Opening a Chestnut Burr* (1874), were annually attracting thousands of new readers. Pamplet editions of these two early novels, originally published ten or more years before, were sold at newstands and on railways—152,000 copies in 1884 alone—without diminishing the steady sales of the hardcover editions.

An Original Belle (1884).   Roe's developing skills and capacities as a novelist are evident in *An Original Belle* (1884). Marian Vosburgh uses her influence over her would-be beaus to help them to be wiser and better men. Instead of his usual romantic plot, Roe changes his fictional pattern and gives his heroine the opportunity to be a substantial person helping others. Of interest in this novel are his descriptions of the Battle of Gettysburg during the Civil War. Once more the former chaplain and cavalryman provides authentic and stirring battle scenes. Just as compelling in their historical accuracy and descriptive drama are his inclusion in *An Original Belle* of mob actions from the New York Draft Riots of 1863. Roe, with his characteristic thoroughness, had studied historical records and made his own efforts in oral history. He was able also to insert his own observations: he had been in New York City in 1863 during the worst of the riots.[9]

Nature's Serial Story (1884)

Nature's Serial Story (1884) is usually referred to by Mary Roe and others who were close to Roe as the novel that he wrote with the greatest pleasure. He dedicated this enjoyable and informative story to his wife, Anna, and the book was originally published by Dodd & Mead with illustrations by W. Hamilton Gibson and F. Dielman. He set the story in his favorite spot on the Hudson River, weaving into the life of a farm family extended discussions of nature in all its forms—birds, trees, flowers, storms—and in all seasons.

He Fell in Love with His Wife (1886). The next novel, *He Fell in Love with His Wife,* published in 1886, is based on a situation Roe had read about in a newspaper: a middle-aged widower, unable to pay for hired help to carry on his farm, went to the county poorhouse and said in effect, "If there's a good woman here who can put up with me, I'll marry her." This became the plot of *He Fell in Love with His Wife,* a moving story of true love finally found by two sincerely good people. Roe's subtle handling of the growing love of the lonely man and the perplexed woman has delicacy in touch and genuine creative value.

The Earth Trembled (1887). *The Earth Trembled* (1887), published in a first edition of at least 25,000, has as its center of interest the Charleston earthquake of 31 August 1886, a disaster that took many lives and made thousands homeless. Roe went to Charleston and saw the effects of the earthquake, just as he did with the Chicago fire for *Barriers Burned Away.* *The Earth Trembled* has historical scope, for Roe begins the novel with the bombardment of Fort Sumter—the opening engagement of the Civil War—and concludes it with scenes from the earthquake. The novel received especially favorable reviews in

England, where even a fourth edition of 34,000 copies sold out quickly. *The Earth Trembled* illustrates Roe's authorial growth, particularly his blend of humor and pathos.

"Miss Lou" (1888). *"Miss Lou"* is Roe's last novel. Though he died before completing it, Dodd & Mead published it with a postscript. They used Roe's notes to explain how the novel ended and how the characters turned out. It is a story of Southern life, and one of Roe's best novels, enjoyable, well plotted, and developed with control and judgment. Miss Lou is a young Southern girl who has been reared to believe that all Yankee soldiers are inhuman brutes. But when the Civil War reaches the plantation where she lives, she learns that Yankees, like Southerners, include both the good and the bad. She then falls in love with a Union soldier.

Roe's Other Writing

Besides his novels Roe wrote several novellas, short stories, and books and pamphlets on horticulture. Some of these have already been commented upon, such as *Play and Profit in My Garden* (1873), *A Manual on the Culture of Small Fruits* (1876), and *Success with Small Fruits* (1880). There were other publications, too.

In *Home Acre* (serialized in *Harper's Magazine* and published by Dodd & Mead in 1889) Roe explains how one should ideally plant one acre. On this acre he utilizes every inch of land, planting fruit trees, raspberries, currants, and strawberries. He explains where grass should be grown, where the gardens should be located, particularly the "kitchen garden," as well as how to design the paths and walkways through the acre. Describing how an amateur can successfully grow vegetables and fruit, Roe exhibits his expert horticultural knowledge as well as his love for the soil and its potential cornucopia.

Roe's novellas and short stories were always snapped up eagerly by periodicals. *The Hornet's Nest, a Story of Love and War* (1887–157 pages) features the American Revolution and is centered in the area around Charlotte, North Carolina, known as "the hornet's nest," especially to Lord Charles Cornwallis, because of the heavy fighting there. The main character is Angus McIntire, and his growth into manhood during the revolution takes up most of this story.

An Unexpected Result and Other Stories (1883) contains three stories: "An Unexpected Result," "Christmas Eve in War Times," "Three Thanksgiving Kisses." After Roe's death two other stories were added in reissues of the book: "Taken Alive" and "Susie Roliffe's Christmas." Roe liked the Christmas season, and he had no rigid fundamental and puritanical beliefs that it should be completely a solemn observance. In these holiday stories Christmas is a time for family pleasures and happy reunions.

Taken Alive and Other Stories (published first in 1889 and again in 1892) capitalizing on Roe's popularity, even after his death, includes " 'A Native Author Called Roe' " (his short autobiography), and the stories "Taken Alive," "Found Yet Lost," "Queen of Spades," "A Christmas-Eve Suit," "Jeff's Treasure," "Caught on the Ebb-Tide," "A Brave Little Quakeress," "An Unexpected Result," "Three Thanksgiving Kisses," and "Susie Roliffe's Christmas." Dodd & Mead's efforts, after Roe's death, to make up for the loss of Roe's yearly fiction can be seen in this collection, as stories have been added to flesh out the volume. Dodd & Mead also published *A Brave Little Quakeress and Other Stories* (published also in 1889 and 1892). There are no new stories in this collection and the reprinted stories are familiar: "A Brave Little Quakeress," "Queen of Spades," "Caught on the Ebb-Tide," "Susie Roliffe's Christmas" and "Jeff's Treasure." Thus his publishers coasted on Roe's continuing popularity.

Chapter Five
E. P. Roe:
The Man and the Writer

Edward Payson Roe died on 11 July 1888. His novels were still selling by the thousands; his publishers estimated that up to 1888 over 1,400,000 copies of his books had been sold, not counting the thousands of copies issued in pirated editions in foreign countries. It is true that Roe's novels are not literary classics, but it is also true that they represent a significant movement in American literature. Because of Roe and others such as J. G. Holland, the American novel became acceptable and respectable reading for millions of Americans. Roe's fiction, with its strong moral and ethical themes, brought the religious novel to its peak. Certain that what he wrote would add interest to his themes of living a good life and having faith in God, he included elements in his novels that are clearly modern in their orientation.

He spoke out for the rights and equality of women in *Without a Home,* severely criticizing the inadequate formal education and practical preparation for life under which they suffered. He also excoriated the inhumane working conditions for shopgirls in city stores, demanding in his fiction that something positive be done at once for improvement. He visited tenements in the city, and his condemnation of unsafe and unsatisfactory housing can also be seen in *Without a Home.* In *Driven Back to Eden* the city family escapes to the country and rediscovers what Roe calls the essential values of life—love, understanding, familial closeness, and awareness of one's own talents and potential—all through an association with nature that the undesirable tenement living had crippled and almost aborted. In *Without a Home* Roe looked into America's and the world's future and saw that drug addiction would be one of society's most virulent evils because it would destroy individuals and families and bring about uncontrollable social problems.

Roe is also a superior historical novelist in his depiction of the Civil War. His battle scenes recounting Gettysburg and Bull Run are outstanding, as are his other war descriptions, including those he wrote as a chaplain for the New York *Evangelist.* For his understanding of war, Roe read history books, campaign accounts, conducted his own interviews, and added to all this information his own personal awareness of military life in garrison and in battle.

Some comment should be made about Roe's inclusion of religion in his novels. The religion that he preached as minister, chaplain, and novelist was consistently the same: Pray to God and trust in His guidance. Follow the leadership of Christ and trust in Him as the ideal model for life. Be good, be honorable, be honest, and be true to your best character traits. Be kind to your fellowman and do not separate yourself from those who are rich and poor, good and evil, educated and uneducated, socially prominent and not. Roe believed that all men and women, even those he called misguided, could by prayer and personal inner discipline restore within themselves the goodness that God endowed them with at birth.

His religion is therefore a practical, everyday kind of religion, and nondenominational. As he explained in 1878, "I . . . have tried to speak of Christianity as a *life* rather than as an 'ism' or system of doctrine."[1] He advised his parishioners and his readers to worship God directly and personally, and not to permit church protocol, ritual, and edifices to become barriers to their own potentially intimate relationship with Christ and God. As Roe's characters trust in God, they simultaneously learn to trust themselves, and their inner lives improve, even if their financial and social positions—some of the outer life that should not overrule the inner—do not change. Some of Roe's characters—such as Dennis Fleet and Christine Ludolph—find that money and social position do not matter as long as their values are constant and steady. Roe's advice thus touches on man's search for the ultimate inner peace of both mind and spirit.

He himself lived this way, for his goodness impressed almost everyone he met, including Julian Hawthorne and Lyman Abbott. Roe firmly believed that life should be just and fair. He spoke out against the lack of an international copyright law, just as he also severely criticized his imitator, E. R. Roe. Yet Roe had most of all a sense of proportion and a sense of humor.

He accepted the many criticisms of his books, saying he realized that he was not writing literary classics but that he was writing what he was capable of writing, hoping that his readers would enjoy and benefit from his novels. He emphasized that he was not imitating any other authors: he was writing the best he could, and he tried to improve with each novel, an achievement that becomes evident as one reads all of his works. Roe no doubt realized that what Emerson wrote about envy being ignorance and imitation being suicide is a true and practical guideline. In all his activities all through his life Roe was his own man.

Roe could laugh along with the readers of *Puck* magazine when it made satirical fun of his cultivation of strawberries and parodied his frequent inclusion of strawberries in many of his novels. *Puck*'s parodic lines concerned "New Fashions in Strawberries," by E. Shad Roe, Newburgh Professor of Strawberries, whose newest strawberry varieties included "Reddy the Blacksmith Round Top Seedling" and "Salathiel Single Twist Prolific."[2] Roe could laugh at himself, and his novels include comedic scenes and witty repartee. In his comments on himself and his writing Roe showed that he was able to evaluate honestly his capacities as a writer.

In some ways Roe is like George MacDonald (1824–1905), the Scottish Congregational minister who also became an author. What C. S. Lewis wrote about MacDonald—that he was primarily a Christian teacher whose writings were full of pulpit oratory and verbosity—can also, unfortunately, be said about Roe. What Lewis wrote further about MacDonald can also be applied to Roe: "If we define Literature as an art whose medium is words, then certainly MacDonald has no place in its first rank—perhaps not even in its second." But Lewis qualifies this judgment, and his comment here could also be made about Roe and his writing: "There are indeed passages, many of them . . . , where the wisdom and (I would dare to call it) the holiness that are in him triumph over and even burn away the baser elements in his style: the expression becomes precise, weighty, economic; acquires a cutting edge."[3]

Lyman Abbott, who had assisted Roe when he was writing the earliest drafts of *Barriers Burned Away,* spoke about Roe— the man, the writer, the minister, the soldier—on Decoration Day, 30 May 1894, when Roe Park was dedicated at Cornwall-on-the-Hudson. In this memorial address Abbott commented: "That fiction is the highest which by the imagination makes real to our thought the common affairs of life, and yet so blends them with noble ideals that we are able to go back into life with a larger, a nobler, and a more perfect faith." Roe in his writings, Abbott added, "ministered to the life not of ten thousand, or of one hundred thousand, but of thousands of thousands, for his readers in this country alone are numbered by the millions." Roe thus enabled many thousands of men and women "to see the beauty and the truth—in one word, the divinity—that there is in human life." In his conclusion Abbott was prescient, saying that Roe was an "inspiration to the higher, nobler and diviner life" in all humankind, and that "time may even obliterate the name of E. P. Roe from the memory of men" but not the values he believed in.[4]

As Abbott accurately predicted, the passage of time has not been kind to the writings of E. P. Roe. He himself recognized this possibility during his lifetime. In his reply to Matthew Arnold he wrote: "No one buys or reads a book under compulsion. . . . When a critic condemns my books, I accept that as his judgment; when another critic and scores of men and women, the peers of the first in cultivation and intelligence, commend the books, I do not charge them with gratuitous lying." In 1888, just before death caught him unawares, he wrote, "My one aim has become to do my work conscientiously and leave the verdict to time and the public. I wish no other estimate than a correct one; and when the public indicate that they have had enough of Roe I shall neither whine nor write" (*NA,* 490).

Roe believed that he should write as well as he was able, and he believed that a novel could be religious yet interesting and enjoyable. "Life in novels, as in men, is of greatly variable duration," and "the living novel is rarely if ever produced by an imitator, a follower, or the disciple of a school"; further, "the living novel may be distinctly religious . . . , [for] the student of life finds religion . . . inextricably interwoven with human experience. . . ."[5]

These are the principles Edward Payson Roe followed when he wrote his novels. They explain why he became not only a best-selling novelist but also a people's writer, America's "native author."

Notes and References

Preface

1. Fred Lewis Pattee, *A History of American Literature* (Boston, 1896), 442–43.
2. Julian Hawthorne, "Edward Payson Roe," *Critic* 10 (28 July 1888):43.
3. Edward Roberts, "How Mr. Roe Impressed His Friends," *Critic* 10 (4 August 1888):49.
4. Paul R. Cleveland, "Is Literature Bread-Winning?" *Cosmopolitan* 5 (June 1888):319.

Chapter One

1. " 'A Native Author Called Roe,' " *Lippincott's Monthly Magazine* 42 (October 1888):493–94, hereafter cited in the text as *NA* followed by page number.
2. Katherine M. Babbitt, "E. P. Roe: A Preliminary Check List," Master's thesis, State University Center at Albany (State University of New York), 3.
3. Ibid., 3–4.
4. Vachel Lindsay, "John L. Sullivan, The Strong Boy of Boston," *Selected Poems of Vachel Lindsay,* ed. Mark Harris (New York: Macmillan, 1964), 13–14.
5. Frank Luther Mott, *Golden Multitudes: The Story of Best Sellers in the United States* (New York, 1947), 148.
6. "Obituary," *Publishers Weekly* 34 (28 July 1888):140.
7. "A Popular Benefactor," *Harper's Bazar* 21 (18 August 1888):52.
8. Matthew Arnold, "Civilization in the United States," *Nineteenth Century* 23 (April, 1888):492.
9. Mary A. Roe, *E. P. Roe, Reminiscences of His Life* (in the same volume with *He Fell in Love with His Wife*) (New York, 1902), 319, hereafter cited as Mary Roe. (Mary A. Roe wrote two novels worth noting: *Forging Their Chains* and *A Long Search.*)
10. Susan Roe, Diary (holograph manuscript). Highland Falls, New York: E. P. Roe Collection of Katherine M. Babbitt, p. 4, hereafter cited as Susan Roe.
11. E. D. Walker, "Edward P. Roe," *Cosmopolitan* 5 (September 1888):401.

12. Susan Roe, 12–13.
13. Ibid., 8.
14. Ibid., 19.
15. Mary Roe, 324.
16. Ibid., 323–24.
17. Susan Roe, 21.
18. Ibid., 20.
19. Ibid., 9.
20. Ibid., 17–18.
21. Mary Roe, 322.
22. Walker, "Edward P. Roe," 402.
23. William S. Walsh, "Some Words about E. P. Roe," *Lippincott's Monthly Magazine* 42 (October 1888):498.
24. Ibid.
25. Susan Roe, 11.
26. Mary Roe, 325.
27. A. Moss Merwin, quoted by Mary Roe, 326–27.
28. Ibid., 327.
29. Ibid.
30. Mary Roe, 329.
31. New York *Tribune*, n.d., quoted by Mary Roe, 329–30.
32. New York *Observer*, n.d., quoted by Mary Roe, 330.
33. *Evangelist*, 30 October 1862, 2.
34. Ibid., 6 November 1862, 2.
35. Ibid., 5 February 1863, 2.
36. Ibid.
37. Ibid.
38. Ibid., 30 October 1862, 2.
39. Ibid., 14 January 1864, 2.
40. Ibid.
41. Ibid.
42. Mary Roe, 328.
43. Ibid., 358.
44. Letter to Mary Roe as quoted by her, 358.
45. *Evangelist*, 27 July 1984, p. 2.
46. Ibid.
47. Roe to William H. Wickham, Private collection of the family of Joseph Wickham Roe, Southport, Conn.
48. "The Element of Life in Fiction," Chicago *Forum* 5 (April 1888):227, 228–29.
49. Ibid., 234, 226.
50. Pattee, *A History of American Literature*, 443.
51. Fred Lewis Pattee, *A History of American Literature since 1870* (New York, 1915), 388.

Chapter Two

1. Newspaper article quoted by Mary Roe, 386.
2. "My First Novel," *Cosmopolitan* 5 (July 1887):328, hereafter cited in the text as *FN* followed by page number.
3. Roe to Lyman Abbott, January 1872, Bowdoin College Library, Brunswick, Maine.
4. Edward H. Dodd, Jr., *The First Hundred Years* (New York, 1939), 17.
5. Ibid., 18.
6. George Ripley, *New York Tribune,* 7 February 1873, 7.
7. Ibid., 6.
8. *Barriers Burned Away* (New York, 1885), 4; hereafter page numbers given in the text in parentheses.

Chapter Three

1. For an excellent consideration of this subject, see C. G. Barker-Benfield's *The Horrors of the Half-Known Life* (New York: Harper & Row, 1976), a thorough consideration of male attitudes toward women and sexuality in nineteenth-century America.
2. *What Can She Do?* (New York, 1873), viii; hereafter page numbers given in the text in parentheses.
3. *Opening a Chestnut Burr* (New York, 1874), p. 8; hereafter page numbers given in the text in parentheses.
4. Roe, as quoted by Mary Roe, 398–99.
5. Dr. Edgar A. Mearns, as quoted by Mary Roe, 399–400.
6. Mary Roe, 401–2.
7. Ibid., 403.
8. Ibid.

Chapter Four

1. Walker, "Edward P. Roe," 401.
2. Mary Roe, 408–9.
3. Roe newspaper interview, as quoted by Mary Roe, 410.
4. William S. Walsh, "Some Words about E. P. Roe," 479.
5. Paul R. Cleveland, "Is Literature Bread-Winning?" *Cosmopolitan* 5 (June 1888):319.
6. "Gentle Woman Roused" (New York: National Temperance Society and Publication House, 1874), 3,1.
7. *Without a Home* (New York, 1881), vii.
8. *His Sombre Rivals* (New York, 1883), iii–iv.
9. *An Original Belle* is a novel worthy of note by literary critics of the American nineteenth century and by Civil War historians.

George Arthur Dunlap in *The City in the American Novel 1789–1900* (New York, 1965), for example, focuses favorable attention on Roe's realistic descriptions of mob violence during these riots.

Chapter Five

1. Letter of 28 November 1878 quoted in "The Writings of E. P. Roe," *Literary World* 19 (4 August 1888):248.

2. E. Shad Roe, "New Fashions in Strawberries," *Puck* 11 (26 April 1882):118.

3. C. S. Lewis, preface to *George MacDonald—An Anthology* (New York: Macmillan, 1978), xxvi.

4. Lyman Abbott, quoted by Mary Roe, 470, 471, 472.

5. "Element of Life," 236, 235.

Selected Bibliography

PRIMARY SOURCES

1. Novels
Barriers Burned Away. New York: Dodd & Mead, 1872. Reprint. 1885.
A Day of Fate. New York: Dodd & Mead, 1880.
The Earth Trembled. New York: Dodd & Mead, 1887.
A Face Illumined. New York: Dodd & Mead, 1877.
Found Yet Lost. New York: Dodd & Mead, 1888.
From Jest to Earnest. New York: Dodd & Mead, 1875.
He Fell in Love with His Wife. New York: Dodd & Mead, 1886.
His Sombre Rivals. New York: Dodd & Mead, 1883.
The Hornet's Nest. New York: Dodd & Mead, 1887.
A Knight of the Nineteenth Century. New York: Dodd & Mead, 1877.
"Miss Lou." New York: Dodd & Mead, 1888.
Nature's Serial Story. New York: Dodd & Mead, 1885.
Near to Nature's Heart. New York: Dodd & Mead, 1876.
Opening a Chestnut Burr. New York: Dodd & Mead, 1874.
An Original Belle. New York: Dodd & Mead, 1885.
What Can She Do? New York: Dodd & Mead, 1873.
Without a Home. New York: Dodd & Mead, 1881.
A Young Girl's Wooing. New York: Dodd & Mead, 1884.

2. Novel for Children
Driven Back to Eden. New York: Dodd & Mead, 1885.

3. Collections of Novellas and Short Stories
A Brave Little Quakeress and Other Stories. New York: Dodd & Mead, 1892.
Queen of Spades, and " 'A Native Author Called Roe.' " Philadelphia: Lippincott, 1888. A special issue of *Lippincott's Monthly Magazine.*
Taken Alive and Other Stories. New York: Dodd & Mead, 1889.
An Unexpected Result and Other Stories. New York: Dodd & Mead, 1883.

4. Horticultural Books and Pamphlets
The Home Acre. New York: Dodd & Mead, 1889.

A Manual on the Culture of Small Fruits. Newburg, New York: Journal
  Printing Establishment, 1874.
Play and Profit in My Garden. New York: Dodd & Mead, 1873.
Success with Small Fruits. New York: Dodd & Mead, 1880.

5. Autobiography
" 'A Native Author Called Roe.' " *Lippincott's Monthly Magazine* 42
  (October 1888):479–97.

6. Other Separate Publications
Birthday Mottoes Selected from the Writings of E. P. Roe [sometimes known
  as *The Roe Birthday Book*]. Edited by Lyman Abbott, 1882.
"Gentle Woman Roused." New York: National Temperance Society
  and Publishing House, 1874.

7. Articles
"The Element of Life in Fiction." *Forum* 5 (April 1888):226–36.
"How to Succeed in Literature." *Home and School Supplement: An Illus-
  trated Educational Monthly,* December 1886, 165–69.
"International Petty Larceny." *Publishers Weekly* 15 (9 January
  1886):47–48.
["Letter to the Editor."] *Literary World* 19 (4 August 1884):248.
"My First Novel: *Barriers Burned Away.*" *Cosmopolitan* 3 (July
  1887):327–29. Reprinted in *Publishers Weekly* 16 (23 July
  1887):77–78.
"The Strawberry in History and Poetry." *Publishers Weekly* 9 (19 June
  1880):627–29.

SECONDARY SOURCES

1. Bibliographical
Babbitt, Katherine M. "E. P. Roe: A Preliminary Check List." Master's thesis, State University Center at Albany, State University
  of New York. The outstanding resource for bibliographical information on E. P. Roe's writings.

2. Biographical
Roe, Mary A. *E. P. Roe: Reminiscences of His Life.* New York: P. F.
  Collier & Sons, 1902. Mary A. Roe's recollections of her brother
  Edward are of genuine value. Useful too because some of Roe's
  Civil War chronicles to the *Evangelist* are included, as well as
  other writings.

Roe, Susan. Diary (holograph manuscript). Highland Falls, New York: E. P. Roe Collection of Katherine M. Babbitt. Invaluable for its insight into the home life of the Roe family and for the early years of E. P. Roe, Susan Roe's brother.

3. Books

Ahlstrom, Sidney E. *A Religious History of the American People.* New Haven: Yale University Press, 1972. A monumental study of religion in America. See especially chapter 50 for a background of religious thought in Roe's day.

Altick, Richard D. *The English Common Reader.* Chicago: University of Chicago Press, 1957. A social history of the general reading public from 1800 to 1900. Helpful in assessing Roe's popularity as a novelist.

Dodd, Edward H., Jr. *The First Hundred Years.* New York: Dodd & Mead, 1939. A history (from 1839 to 1939) of Dodd & Mead, the publishers of Roe's books. *Barriers Burned Away* specifically considered as a best-selling phenomenon.

Dunlap, George Arthur. *The City in the American Novel, 1789–1900.* New York: Russell & Russell, 1965. Praises Roe for his realistic depiction of the 1863 New York City Draft Riots in *An Original Belle.*

Gosse, Edmund. *Questions at Issue.* London: Heinnemann, 1893. Discusses Roe's achievements as a popular author; notes that his novels were neglected by America's "lettered classes."

Howe, Daniel Walker, ed. *Victorian America.* Philadelphia: University of Pennsylvania Press, 1976. Of genuine value for presenting an overall perspective of Victorian values and practices.

Mott, Frank Luther. *Golden Multitudes: The Story of Best Sellers in the United States.* New York: Macmillan, 1947. Gives specific information about the phenomenal sales of Roe's novels.

Mumford, Lewis. *The Brown Decades.* New York: Dover, 1955. Excellent background for the period when Roe's novels were being published.

Pattee, Fred Lewis. *A History of American Literature.* Boston: Silver, Burdett & Co., 1896. Pattee's first evaluation of Roe's fiction and why it appealed to millions of readers in America, Canada, England, and elsewhere.

———. *A History of American Literature since 1870.* New York: Century Co., 1915. Pattee's analysis of Roe's fiction is significant and still useful.

———. *The New American Literature: 1890–1930.* New York: Cooper Square Publishers, 1968. Originally published in 1930.

Reynolds, David S. *Faith in Fiction: The Emergence of Religious Literature in America.* Cambridge, Mass.: Harvard University Press, 1981. Full-length analysis of American religious fiction from 1776 to 1850. Also discusses Roe and his contemporaries.

Van Doren, Carl. *The American Novel: 1789–1939.* New York: Macmillan, 1940. Gives Roe and J. G. Holland credit for bringing about the acceptance of the novel by middle-class America.

Wilson, John F. *Public Religion in American Culture.* Philadelphia: Temple University Press, 1979. Excellent monograph on the interpretation of public religion in America. Helpful in understanding the influence of Roe's novels on the American social milieu.

4. Articles

Abbott, John S. C. "The Military Hospitals at Fortress Monroe." *Harper's New Monthly Magazine* 29 (August 1864):306–22. Roe served as a chaplain during the Civil War at Fort Monroe.

Arnold, Matthew. "Civilization in the United States." *Nineteenth Century* 23 (April 1888):481–96. A seminal statement on Roe.

Boyesen, H. H. "American Literary Criticism and Its Value." *Forum* 15 (June 1893):459–66. Discusses Roe and J. G. Holland.

Browne, Julius Henri. "The Manuscript Market." *Forum* 1 (July 1886):477–85. Helpful in assessing Roe's success as a best-selling religious novelist.

Cleveland, Paul R. "Is Literature Bread-Winning?" *Cosmopolitan* 5 (June 1888):312–20. Discusses Roe's book royalties.

"Edward Payson Roe." *Critic* 10 (28 July 1888):43. Useful as an assessment at Roe's death of the contemporary importance of his fiction and the remarkable sale of his books.

"Edward Payson Roe." *Every Other Saturday* 2 (1 August 1885):242–43. Discusses the success of Roe's novels.

Hawthorne, Julian. "Edward Payson Roe." *Critic* 10 (28 July 1888):43–44. A touching and sincere tribute.

"Literary Notes." *Life* 6 (10 September 1885):142. Good satire on Twain, James, Howells, and Roe.

Mabie, Hamilton W. "The Most Popular Novels in America." *Forum* 16 (December 1893):508–16. Assesses and lists novel sales, showing Roe's high rankings.

Maurice, Arthur Bartlett. "Best Sellers of Yesterday: E. P. Roe's *Barriers Burned Away.*" *Bookman* 33 (May 1911):247–53. Discusses the 1910 presentation of *Barriers Burned Away* as a play at the Bijou Opera House, Minneapolis, Minnesota.

Minor, Dennis E. "The New and Regenerated Adams of E. P. Roe." *Markham Review* 6 (Winter 1977):21–26. Fine interpretation of

Barriers Burned Away and *Opening a Chestnut Burr.* Connects the
  themes of these two early Roe novels to the theme of *The Great
  Gatsby* and similar modern American fiction.
"A Popular Benefactor." *Harper's Bazar* 21 (18 August 1888):52.
  Obituary and critical assessment.
Roberts, Edward. "How Mr. Roe Impressed His Friends." *Critic*
  (4 August 1888):49. Moving praise.
Roe, E. Shad [pseudonym]. "New Fashions in Strawberries." *Puck*
  11 (26 April 1882):118. A satire on Roe's use of strawberries
  in his novels, as well as his horticultural publications.
Walsh, William S. "Some Words about E. P. Roe." *Lippincott's
  Monthly Magazine* 42 (October 1888):497–500. Excellent on Roe
  the man.

Index